MW01488232

LIVING in
the BLESSING:

Experiencing God's Promise for
All who Hear and Obey His Word

BOOK 1
RECEIVING
the
BLESSING

Dr. Chet Taylor

Copyright © 2021 Chet Taylor

ISBN: 9798752096471

DEDICATION

In Memory of

Mary Louise McDonald

Her life of grace has greatly blessed me and has moved me to share the grace she lived in with all who wish to live in His blessing.

TABLE OF CONTENTS

Acknowledgements

The themes in this series of books were first introduced to the church family I served for over thirty-three years, Lakeview Fellowship of Fort Worth, TX. I have very fond memories of the times we shared together, especially on Wednesday nights, pouring over the Scriptures, praying together, and encouraging each other. My sincerest thanks go out to each one who shared in this journey with me—and who encouraged me to continue in it.

I am also very grateful to the board and those who serve on the team of "Living in the Blessing Ministries." Your support, labor, and belief in this project have meant more than you know. Christy Dodson, thanks for your help with cover design. Pat Uttz, thanks for your labor to format the books. Barbara Harlan, thank you for reading through the chapters and for your incredibly helpful input. Randy Maynard, as you have taught these materials to others, your feedback and your encouragement have greatly inspired me. Scott Athey, to serve with you over many years has been a great joy. Our visits over the content of these books have been a great help too. Donny and Tracy Spurlock, the support you have provided has been invaluable, and to Tracy's mom, the late Barbara Sarrels, I want to express my deepest gratitude. Wayne McDonald, all of the kindness, grace, and support that you and your beloved Mary Louise have shown me, over many years, is beyond what I can express.

As I think about so many who have proofed chapters, prayed, and provided such helpful counsel, I can only express my sincerest gratitude. I pray you will know that God sees and knows everything you have done, and my heart's desire is that you will sense His smile over you.

Above all, I have no greater supporter, friend, or encourager than my wife, Jeanie. Many times she has asked me: "Is the book ready yet?" My only answer has been, "The more I work on it, the more it works on me." I just didn't realize how much work was needed—on me, and

I'm only beginning to see how much work still needs to be done. I count myself blessed to be included among the world of people who are touched by the grace she continually shows.

Together, we want to express our love and gratitude to each of our children, Blake, Brittany, and Breanna—and all of their families. You are all a great blessing to us, beyond what you can know, and our deepest prayer is that you know and live in the fullness of God's blessing for you.

Introduction

One day, as Jesus was speaking to a crowd, a woman was so moved by His words she cried out: "Blessed is the womb that bore You, and blessed are the breasts that nursed You!" Jesus replied by saying: "Blessed rather are those who hear the word of God and obey it (Luke 11:27-28)."

When I first read these verses, I thought, "Now that seems like a really random thing for someone to say while Jesus was teaching...." However, Jesus didn't see it that way. He knew this woman was genuinely moved, as so many were, by His words, and the thing He was most eager to express was that *anyone* who hears and obeys God's word can be blessed. Without question, Jesus' mother was incredibly blessed to be the one to bear the life of the Messiah and to nurture Him. However, the reason she was so blessed was because she herself heard and obeyed God's word (Luke 1:38, 45). And this is the theme of this entire discipleship curriculum:

God holds out the promise of blessing for all who will hear and obey His word.

The connection between discipleship and God's blessing is not hard to see. A disciple is a "learner" or "follower." Jesus said in Matt. 10:27: "My sheep listen to My voice; I know them, and they follow Me." This is what a disciple does, and this is what God promises to bless. Therefore, the path to true blessing is discipleship, and the beautiful thing about this is that God's blessings move us all the more to live as His disciples.

This leads me to the passion behind this series of books. It begins with what I have experienced in my own journey.

To give just a few examples, as I have endeavored to live on the basis of hearing and obeying, I have noticed that my life has not become busier. Just the opposite, it has actually become quite simpler, and this is because so many of things that I was doing were not things that God spoke at all.

There was a time when I saw discipleship primarily as "discipline." And discipline is certainly useful in many realms of our lives. However, the true essence of discipleship is not discipline, as helpful as it may be (1 Tim. 4:7-8). You can be a highly disciplined person without being a disciple. A disciple hears and obeys the voice of God. This is what brings God's blessing, and this is the greatest discipline of a disciple.

And there is something else I have discovered. I remember very clearly a Tuesday morning, when I was praying with a group of men. One of my prayers was that God would reveal what He wanted me to share the following Sunday. As I waited, I had this overwhelming sense that God was saying: "I just want them to know how much I love them."

I was deeply moved by this, not just because it revealed what He wanted me to say the following Sunday, but because it revealed to me the heart God carries toward all of us *always*. In all honesty, my tendency is to fear what God would speak to me. What would God require of me? And will I be able to do it? I have come to see that these questions are rooted in my own lack of faith. Every time God has been merciful enough to allow me to hear His voice, the effect on me has been just the opposite. I am overwhelmed with the gentleness and love in His voice. And every time I obey, even when it seems very challenging to me, the fruit is always blessing.

This has brought me to realize that, if I fear what He would speak, it is because of my own lack of faith—and because I don't yet know Him as He truly is. It's something I'm still growing in, but my experience has been this: with every word He speaks, I love and trust Him more. This is because all of His ways are "loving and faithful" (Ps.

25:10) and he alone possesses "the words of eternal life" (John 6:68).

And there is another reason for the passion behind these books. I'm thinking now about a man I have great respect for. One evening he shared with me how he was searching for what he could do in the new season of his life. He had just retired, and he couldn't think of any way he could be of use to others. This surprised me, because I knew of many ways God had touched him, and I had observed how many people were touched by his life. Immediately, I thought, "You can make disciples!" With the wealth of experiences he had, and with the time now available to him, what greater thing could he do? And this is something we can all do. In the last words we have from Jesus in the book of Matthew, He said:

All authority in heaven and on earth has been given to Me. Therefore go and make disciples of all nations, baptizing them in the name of the Father, and of the Son, and of the Holy Spirit, and teaching them to obey all that I have commanded you. And surely I am with you always, even to the end of the age." (Matt. 28:18-20)

The reason we can all make disciples is because Jesus would never tell us to do anything we can't do—with the power He gives us to do it. And this is something we *will* do if we are His disciples, because this is what His disciples do. And the truth of matter is that, if we are His true disciples we can't help but do this. The blessing He pours into our lives will be too great to keep to ourselves.

And there is still another reason for the passion. Have you ever thought to yourself, "What is going on in our world? There is strife, depression, homelessness, hopelessness and on and on." And have you ever asked: "What could I ever do that would make any difference in this world?"

I feel this way sometimes, and I am always drawn to the same conclusion: The only thing that will ever make a difference in our world is precisely what Jesus told us to do from the very start:

We must make disciples.

I have this picture in my mind of the apostle Paul, on the day he first set foot in the city of Corinth. It was around the year 51 AD, during his second missionary journey. The city of Corinth was known for its blatant immorality. In fact, even to this day, if you consult a dictionary, whether in hand or online, you will find a definition for "corinithinize." It means "to live a promiscuous life."

What then did Paul say when he first entered the city? Did he say, "Look at what the world is coming to!" I don't think so. I think he said, "Look who's come to the world!"

And this must be the spirit we carry and the message we share, because the message and its power are still the same, and above all else, this is the mission of these four short books. It is to convey this same message.

The first book is called, **Receiving the Blessing**. We will never live in God's blessing until we first receive it, and before we can receive it, we must trust the heart of the One who gives it. This is why this book focuses so much on knowing and trusting God's true nature.

The next book is, **Growing in the Blessing**. Here you will find some of the basic topics that are part of many discipleship curriculums. We will begin with what it means to hear and to obey. Then we will look at the things we need to do to position ourselves to hear what God speaks. We will also look at the fruit that comes from hearing and obeying, which is also the evidence that we are growing more and more to hear and obey God's voice.

The third book is called, **Guarding the Blessing**. As we learn to live in God's blessing, we must guard it. In this book I am especially eager to convey the blessing we can live in even in the midst of the deepest trials we endure.

The fourth book is: ***Multiplying the Blessing***. Multiplication is a part of God's created order, and it is the means by which Jesus' closest disciples had such great impact in the world. It remains His strategy for the great needs of our world today.

From a practical standpoint, there are discussion questions at the end of each chapter. The purpose for these is to facilitate interaction.

You might be thinking: "Is this a tool I can use to make disciples?" And if so, you may also be asking: "Who can I share these materials with?" I certainly pray you can use this curriculum for that purpose, but I would actually encourage you to begin with the opposite question: "Who can disciple me?" And with that question: "Who can I pursue to invest in my life?"

I say this because we have to receive before we can give. In the work of making disciples, we need the encouragement and counsel of those who pour into our lives first. If you already have this support, especially through the nurture and oversight of those who shepherd His Church, then, by all means, I pray this tool will be of use. It will be a greater tool, though, when you are able to pour into others out of what is poured into you.

All the Scripture citations, unless otherwise indicated, are taken from the Berean Study Bible. I like the name of this translation. It was during Paul's second missionary journey that he also came to a town called Berea. According to Acts 17:11, the people of this town were "noble-minded" because they carefully evaluated Paul's teachings to see if they were consistent with the Scriptures. This is my great encouragement to you as well. Please evaluate everything you read in the pages that follow in the light of Scriptures.

As you do this, I pray you will grow to know, not just the words

God has spoken, but the God who has spoken them—and every blessing He gives. Most of all, if you are moved to bless the God of heaven
for the blessings He has given you, I will consider myself most greatly
blessed.

Chet Taylor
Fort Worth, TX
2021

CHAPTER 1

What it Means to be Blessed

We hear the word "bless" a lot—or some form of it. I've heard professional athletes talk about how "blessed" they are to play the game they love. We see the word "blessed" on T Shirts and ball caps. We say "the blessing" before meals, and we pray God will "bless" those we care about. We hear politicians close their speeches with "God bless you …."

This brings up a very important question though. Just what does it mean to be blessed? If we are going to live in God's blessing, it only makes sense that we need to understand what it actually is.

So where do we begin?

I don't know of a better place than with the blessing God instructed the priests to speak over the Israelites during Old Testament times. We find this in Num. 6:22-26:

Then the LORD said to Moses, "Tell Aaron and his sons: This is how you are to bless the Israelites. Say to them:

'May the LORD bless you
 and keep you;

may the LORD cause His face to shine upon you
 and be gracious to you;

may the LORD lift up His countenance toward you
 and give you peace.'

God called Aaron and his sons (and their descendants after them) to serve as priests in Israel. This is why this blessing is commonly called "The Aaronic Blessing" or "The Priestly Blessing." The role of a priest was to represent God before the people and the people before God, and in this case, they were to represent God before the people. This was not a prayer they offered to God on behalf of the people; it was a blessing they spoke over the people on behalf of God.

It's important to make this distinction because this blessing was not something the priests or the people had to draw out of God, as if He was reluctant to give it. It was initiated by God, so it expressed the desire and very longing of His heart. What then can we learn from the Priestly Blessing about what it means to be blessed?

Let's begin with the meaning of the word "bless" itself.

The Meaning of the Word "Bless"

In the original Hebrew, the word translated "bless" in the Priestly Blessing is the word *barak* (baw-rak'), which means "to kneel." We see an example of this in Ps. 95:6:

O come, let us worship and bow down;
 let us kneel [*barak*] before the LORD our Maker.

This word is used to speak of the blessing God gives us as well as the blessing we give Him. In Ps. 29:11 we read:

The LORD gives His people strength;
 the LORD blesses [*barak*] His people with peace.

And Ps. 34:1 speaks of the blessing we give to God:

I will bless [*barak*] the LORD at all times;
 His praise will always be on my lips.

This brings up another question though. How could God ever bless us in the sense of kneeling before us? We understand how we should kneel before Him, but for Him to kneel before us sounds backwards to us and even inappropriate....

To understand this, we need to go back to creation itself. In the very first verse of the Bible, we learn that God created the heavens and the earth (Gen. 1:1). Then He fashioned everything He created (Gen. 1:2-25), and He did this to provide a habitat for us, those He created in His image (Gen. 1:26-27). Therefore, as hard as it may be for us to fathom, when God created the heavens and the earth, He bowed low to bless us with the gift of our lives and the creation we live in. And this is what moves us to bow before Him and to bless Him in return.

One way for us to see both sides of this blessing is in the simple prayer the Jewish people have prayed before their meals for many generations:

Blessed are You, O Lord our God, King of the universe,
 who brings forth bread from the earth.

In our day, it's common for us to ask God to "bless our food." However, the prayer above is not a prayer to ask God to *bless our food*; *it is a prayer to bless God for the food*. He is the One who blesses us by bringing forth bread from the earth, and the purpose of the prayer is to bless Him for the blessing He has given us.

One reason we may struggle to understand how God could kneel before us is because we tend to think the lesser should bow before the greater. However, we might think of a father who bends down to interact with his children in some way. It

> When God blesses us, the infinitely greater bows low to serve us, aid us, or benefit us in some way.

may be to feed them, bathe them, clothe them, play with them, etc. This is the picture we need to see if we are going to understand the biblical concept of blessing. When God blesses us, the infinitely greater bows low to serve us, aid us, or benefit us in some way.

The Language of the Priestly Blessing

Just as we can learn much from the Hebrew word for "bless" (*barak*) in the Priestly Blessing, there is much we can learn from the language of the entire blessing. After speaking God's blessing over the people ("May the LORD bless you…"), the priests were to continue

> He longs to keep us, not just from harm, but for Himself.

by saying: "… and keep you." This is the language of protection, and as is the case with all protection, it includes not just *protection from*, but *protection for*. He longs to keep us, not just from harm, but for Himself. He literally wants to "keep" us.

Then, the blessing continues: "May the LORD cause His face to shine upon you…." In Scripture, light in one's face expresses favor. For example, in Pr. 16:15 we read:

> When a king's face brightens, there is life;
>   his favor is like a rain cloud in spring.[1]

---

[1] For other examples, see Ps. 44:3, 67:1 and 89:15-18.

The word for "favor" in this verse is based on the Hebrew word *ratsah* (raw-tsaw'), which means, "to be pleased with." God's favor is His acceptance of us and His being entirely for us, but most of all, it is His pleasure in us. We find favor with God when He finds pleasure in us.

We might wonder how God could find pleasure in us, given everything He knows about us, and we find the reason in what comes next: "… and be gracious to you." In the original Hebrew, this word "gracious" is *chanan* (khaw-nan'). It also refers to favor, but more specifically to "unmerited favor."

Interestingly, this word is similar to *barak* (to bless) in that it means "to descend."[2] In this case, it refers to the act of descending low to show *compassion* on the helpless or *mercy* on those who don't deserve it.[3]

For the sake of clarity, *ratsah* is *merited favor*. It is the favor God shows us because He finds pleasure in us; *chanan* is *unmerited favor*. It is the favor He shows out of His compassion and mercy toward us.

To give a picture of the difference between the two, suppose you come across a homeless person. He is in a helpless condition, and he might be there because of some poor decisions he has made. Out of your *compassion* and *mercy* you decide to give him a place to stay, and you even give him a job in a business you own. This would be an expression of *chanan* (unmerited favor). Then, suppose he is so grateful, he works very hard for you, so much so that you are pleased with his work and decide to give him a promotion. This would be an expression of *ratsah* (merited favor). And there is a very important relationship

---

[2] By way of comparison, the word *chanah* is used for pitching a tent or encamping (Ps. 34:7), which are acts of settling *down*.
[3] See 2 Kings 13:25, Ps. 4:1, 25:16, 26:11, 86:16, Pr. 14:21, Is. 30:18.

between the two. God's unmerited favor (*chanan*) is what moves us to please Him and to live in a way that merits His favor (*ratsah*).

To take this a step further, *unmerited favor* depends on qualities in the one who gives it (compassion and mercy). *Merited favor* depends based on qualities in the one who receives it (a heart and life that brings pleasure).

The reason God is able to show us favor when we don't deserve it is because of His own nature. Thankfully, He is able to see beyond the exterior of our lives into the inner place He made for Himself. And He is able to see us, not just as we are, but as we, by His grace, can become.

God's grace doesn't depend on its object (us); it depends on its source (His own nature). This is why He is able to "cause" His face to shine upon us.

> God's grace doesn't depend on its object (us); it depends on its source (His own nature).

The Priestly Blessing continues: May the LORD lift up His countenance upon you...." The word "countenance" comes from the same word as "face" in the previous verse: *panim* (paw-neem'). Not only does God want us to experience His face shining on us, He wants it to be lifted up over us so it shines on us continually.

Finally, the blessing ends with "... and give you peace." The word "peace" is *shalom* (shaw-lome'), which is more than the absence of conflict or trouble in our lives. It means "completeness" or "soundness." Peace is a function of righteousness (Ps. 85:10, Heb. 12:11), which basically means to be "rightly aligned." This includes our being rightly aligned with God, with the creation He placed us in, and with those we share his creation with—including ourselves. And I need to explain the relationship between peace and grace in the Priestly Blessing. Let's start with this visual:

May the LORD bless you	and keep you;
may the LORD cause His face to shine upon you	and be gracious to you;
may the LORD lift up His countenance toward you	and give you peace.

I have arranged the Priestly blessing this way so you can see the relationship between each part. Many verses in the Bible are given in parallel. Usually, it is just two lines that complement each other or contrast with each other or build on each other. This is to provide a more complete meaning. Here, there are three lines, which only emphasizes how important these words are to the heart of God. In this case, one line *builds* on the other.

In the left column, the second line builds on the first. The true essence of the blessing is the favor we experience from God: He causes His face to shine upon us. Then, in the third line, this favor only expands. He wants it be more than what we receive; He wants it to be what we live in continually.

In the right column, let's start at the end. The peace we experience comes from His grace. And this is such a critical thing for us to understand. Our tendency is to think, "If I can only align my life with God, then He will accept me." And God says, "No, come to me first, and I will align you." His very nature is to show compassion on the helpless and mercy on those who don't deserve it, so we come to Him first. And to understand both of these, grace and peace, we have to go back to the first thing: "and keep you."

Here is something interesting about the word shalom. It comes from another Hebrew word, shalam (shaw-lam'), which is used for "making amends." This refers to the mending, reconciling, aligning, etc. that are necessary to produce the soundness or completeness of shalom. This word, shalam, also carries the connotation of being "safe." When we are not rightly aligned, we are not safe. Our lack of alignment produces in us a debt and makes us vulnerable to others, creation, and ultimately God, so what is the first thing God does? He "keeps us" in the sense of making us safe. His first order of business is to save us. This is the first order of business in all the realms of life, whether in a nation, a school, a home, etc. There must be safety or security.

This is what God does first, but then He knows we continue to need His grace, and our experience of His grace is what give us peace. This is what we see in the New Testament. One of the most common greetings we see from the authors of the New Testament is "Grace to you and peace…." (e.g. 1 Cor. 1:3). Our peace comes from God's grace, and both come from the security of the God who saves and keeps us.

With this foundation in place, God wants us to grow in our alignment with Him in every aspect of our lives, but here is what we have to understand. We are not doing this with the hope of somehow becoming worthy of His grace; we are doing it to be worthy of the grace He has already given. The grace comes first. If we are trying to align our lives to achieve His acceptance, it will result in frustration, bondage, and what we might call "empty religion." However, if we align our lives because of the grace He has given, the result is freedom, power— *peace.*

And yes, it's our lack of peace that tells us there is alignment that needs to take place. If you have ever had a back that is out of alignment, you know your body can speak to you. And our souls can speak to us when we are out of alignment. God wants us to come into alignment with Him so we experience the fullness of His peace, but He does this by demonstrating His grace to us first.

Defining the Blessing

In the Priestly Blessing, we see a close relationship between *blessing* and *favor* (the light of His face). With this in mind, here is a simple definition for "a blessing":

A blessing is a gift God gives as an expression of His favor.

There are a few things in this definition that call for further comment. First, this *favor* can be merited or unmerited. We experience the light of God's face in both, and it's important to remember the relationship between the two. God's unmerited favor moves us to please Him and to live in a way that merits His favor.

Second, we tend to think of "gifts" as material things, but God's blessings are not limited to tangible things alone. We can experience God's blessings in the mere words He speaks to us, as is the case in the Priestly Blessing, and we can experience His blessing in nothing more than His presence with us. His blessings consist of anything (material, relational, spiritual, etc.) that moves us to experience His favor.

Third, the true essence of God's blessing is in our experience of His favor. It's important to emphasize this because God's gifts never become true blessings to us until we actually *experience* His favor in them. Therefore, it's helpful to add this definition:

To be blessed is to experience God's favor in the gifts He gives.

There are many people who possess much of what the world considers valuable, but they don't feel blessed because they don't recognize the things they have as coming from God's hand. Therefore, they experience no sense of God's favor in the things they possess. On the other hand, there are many who possess very little in this world, but they feel greatly blessed because they see what they have as coming from God, and this is what causes them to experience His favor in the gifts He gives.

I remember one of the most distinct times I felt this sense of God's blessing. I had just been called to serve as the pastor of the church I served for over thirty-three years. It was all very new to me. I had never done anything like this before, and I was nervous about it. Would the people accept me? What would my relationship with them be like? Was all of this really going to work out?

One of the first events at the church was their annual 4th of July picnic. At the time, my wife was expecting our first child, so they used the occasion to give us a baby shower. One of the gifts came in a small box. It was a picture of a rocking chair, and it was their way of saying they wanted us to find whatever rocking chair we wanted, and they would pay for it. I know this may not seem like an extremely huge thing, but it was huge for us. Their gift made us feel "blessed." It was not so much the gift as it was what they communicated *in* the gift. It was as if they were saying, "We accept you. We are for you. We are glad you are here." But even more, it was as if God was saying, "This comes from my favor."

And this is what moves all of us to experience His blessing. The inner sense of God's favor *in our hearts* actually means more to us than the gifts He places *in our hands*. It's just that He uses the gifts He gives (of all kinds) to produce in us the experience of His heart toward us.

And that's the blessing….

So far, our focus has been on the meaning of the word "bless" in the Priestly Blessing and the language of the entire blessing. There is more we can learn though from the characteristics we see in God's blessings throughout Scripture.

Primary Characteristics of God's Blessings

More than We Can Accomplish

We can never boast in the blessings God gives us, except to boast in Him, because the true essence of God's blessings is not in what we do; it's in what He does for us. And this is not to say we have no part in the blessings God gives. For example, before the people blessed God for the bread on their tables, they first had to cultivate the soil, plant the seed, and harvest the fields, but they also realized there was nothing they could do apart from what God had already done.

And there is another way they experienced God's blessing. When they honored Him with their obedience, He added to what they did as an expression of His favor. One of the clearest ways we see this is in the contrast between a blessing and its opposite counterpart in Scripture: a curse. Just before the Israelites entered the Promised Land, He said to them:

I have set before you life and death, blessing and cursing. Therefore choose life, so that you and your descendants may live, and that you may love the LORD your God, obey Him, and hold fast to Him. For He is your life…. (Deut. 30:19-20)

Earlier in the book of Deuteronomy, God spells out the specific blessings the people would experience for their obedience, and the curses that would come for their disobedience. And the significant thing for us to observe is that both went beyond the natural result of the things they did.

For example, if they obeyed Him, He would protect their crops and multiply them beyond the natural result of what they did (Deut. 28:1-14), but if they did not obey, the consequences would go beyond the natural result of their disobedience (Deut. 28:15-68). And this didn't mean the effects of the curse were irreversible. God was disciplining them out of His love for them so they would return to Him and the life of blessing He held out for them (Mal. 3:7, 9-12).

A blessing is a "gift" God gives as an expression of His favor, and yes, this requires our part to hear and obey, but when we do this, we are merely positioning ourselves to receive the blessings He gives. Therefore, whether the blessing is in what God has already done before we do anything—or in what He adds to what we do, it's always more than anything we can do.

When the God of heaven bows low to bless us, He does for us what we can't do for ourselves, and when He does this, we never have any inclination to say: "Look at what I did!" We are only moved to say: "Look at what God did for me!"

> we never have any inclination to say: "Look at what I did!"

More than We Can Deserve

I remember teaching on this subject one day when a woman in our group raised her hand to ask: "But what if I just don't deserve to be blessed?" Here is one of the most important things we can understand about the nature of God's blessings. Not only are they more than we can accomplish, they are more than we can deserve.

As we saw earlier, the very heart of the Priestly Blessing is grace ("and be gracious to you"), and this grace is *unmerited favor*. Therefore, it is not something we can earn or deserve. If we are laboring to deserve God's grace, we are seeking it on the wrong basis. It's not just that we don't deserve it; we can't.

What then must we do? Because God's grace is not something we can earn, we can only rely on Him to do for us what we cannot do for ourselves, and we do this by faith (Eph. 2:8-9).

What, then, was the solution for the woman in our group who believed she didn't deserve to be blessed? In a word, it was faith. By faith, we receive the grace of God. Then, as we have seen, God's grace (unmerited favor) is what moves us to please Him and to live in a way that merits His favor, which only increases our sense of God's blessing in the favor we experience from Him. However, even when we are moved to merit God's favor, we can never forget that it was grace that first moved us.

Going back to the illustration of the homeless man, because of the mercy you showed him, he works hard to please you, and this wins your favor, but even when he begins to merit your favor, he can never forget the unmerited favor you first showed him. And the truth of the matter is that, because of the human frailty we all share, he will continue to need your grace. And so it is with us. Even when we are moved to merit God's favor, we can never forget that grace first moved us, and there will never come a time, in this life, when we stop needing it. Therefore, when God blesses us, even out of His pleasure with us, we are never inclined to say, "Look at what I deserved!" We can only say, "This was far more than could have ever earned or deserved...."

we are never inclined to say: "Look at what I deserved!"

No matter what we do, God's blessings are always more than anything we can accomplish or deserve. This is what moves us to sense His favor and to *experience* His blessing. And there is another characteristic of God's blessings.

More than we can Contain

When God blesses us, a beautiful thing happens. We can't keep it to ourselves. We have to respond somehow, and there are two ways we do this. First, we respond upwardly in our praise and thanksgiving to God. And second, we respond outwardly by becoming instruments

of His blessings in the lives of others. Both of these responses are evidences we have received God's blessing, and apart from them His
blessings in our lives will never be complete. There is much more we
need to learn about both of these responses. For now though, may I
encourage you to do two things?

First of all, perhaps it is common for you to count your blessings.
I hope you do this. I don't know of any better attitude to have than an
attitude of gratitude. The next time you count your blessings though,
could I encourage you to do it in a way you may not have done it before? See each one as coming from the eternal God who bows low to
bless us.

See all of creation this way, and then, see the individual aspects of
His creation this way, including the things we tend to take for granted.
See Him bowing low to bless you in the air you breathe, the light by
which you see, the bread on your table….

And the second thing is this. As you count your blessings this way,
allow your heart to experience His favor in each one. And for now, let
your focus simply be on receiving. Why? It's not that our response is
not important (both upward and outward); it is very important. However, we simply can't respond to what we haven't received, and we
can't respond fully to what we haven't received fully. And if we will
fully receive, we won't have to produce any response, because the favor we experience in the blessings God gives will produce the response.

And in this spirit of *receiving*, there is just one more thing I want to
emphasize. As we have seen, the word used for "gracious" in the
Priestly Blessing, *chanan*, means to descend to have *compassion* on the
helpless and *mercy* on those who don't deserve it. And interestingly, not
only is this the word used to express God's grace to us, it is used to
express our cry to God for His grace.

For example, when King Solomon dedicated the Temple, he placed a request before the God of heaven. If there came a time when the people found themselves in a desperate situation because of their sins, if they would repent and plead with God for His aid, his prayer was that God would show them mercy and rescue them (1 Kings 8:47), and the word he used for "plead" is this word *chanan*.

What does this mean? If the people were going to receive God's grace, they had to present a heart to Him that was able to receive it. To say this another way, they had to come to Him with hearts that were able to ask God for His aid even though they didn't deserve it.

In the attempt to convey the meaning of *barak*, the Hebrew word for "bless," I gave you the picture of a father who bows to aid his children in some way. And if this is the posture the father takes, what is the posture we must take?

Have you ever noticed how easy it is for children to acknowledge their needs? But it's not always easy for us. And if we find it difficult, we would do well to hear the words of the apostle Peter in 1 Pet. 5:5:

God opposes the proud,
> but gives grace to the humble.

Are you facing something that seems hopeless? And does this make you feel helpless? Is it hard to ask for God's aid because you don't feel like you deserve it? If so, there is something God wants you to hear. It comes from His own heart. He wants you to hear Him say:

I am a gracious God!. I show compassion to the helpless and mercy to those who don't deserve it.

With this in mind, would you allow His words of blessing to be spoken over you, hopefully with a better understanding of what they mean, and most importantly with the heart to receive them.

His heart never changes, and the same words the priests spoke over the people of Israel are the words He wants you to hear:

May the LORD Bless you
> And keep you;

may the LORD cause His face to shine upon you,
> And be gracious to you;

may the LORD lift up His countenance toward you,
> And give you peace.

Summary

- The word "bless" in the Priestly Blessing comes from the Hebrew word *barak*, which means "to kneel." This gives us a picture of what God does when He blesses us, and this is what moves us to bless Him in return.
- A blessing is a gift He gives as an expression of His favor, and to be blessed is to experience His favor in the gifts He gives.
- God's blessings are more than we can accomplish, more than we deserve, and more than we can contain.
- A blessing produces in us an upward response of praise and thanksgiving and an outward response of blessing others as we have been blessed. Both of these responses are evidences we have received His blessing, and apart from them, His blessing will never be complete in us.
- As important as it is to respond to God's blessing, we cannot respond until we first receive. Therefore, our first priority must be to receive His blessing.
- In order to receive God's grace, we must present to Him a heart that is able to receive it. This is a heart that is willing to

rely on Him to do for us what we cannot do for ourselves even though we don't deserve it.

Discussion Questions
for Chapter 1

1. Are there specific ways God spoke to you through this chapter?

2. What is the meaning of the word "bless" (*barak*) in Num. 6:24?

   Barak = _____ _____

3. What were the definitions given for a) a blessing and b) what it means to be blessed:

a) A blessing is a _____ God gives as an _____
   of His _____

b) To be blessed is to _____
   God's _____
   in the _____ He gives.

4. Can you think of a time when you experienced a true blessing from God—one in which you sensed His favor in a gift you received or a good thing that happened to you? If so, what was it, and how did this blessing affect you?

5. What is the difference between a blessing and a curse? Why does God allow a person to experience a curse? Can you think of a time when you felt as if God was disciplining you for something and calling you back to Him? Based on Heb. 12:5-11, what is God's purpose for disciplining us?

6. What are three primary characteristics of God's blessings?

   More than we can _____

   More than we _____

   More than we can _____

7. What are the two ways we are moved to respond ("more than we can contain") when we receive a true blessing from God?

   _____.

   _____.

8. Do you feel helpless about something right now? If so, what is it? Would you call out to God to help you, even if you don't feel like you deserve it? Would you be willing to share this with others so they can pray for you too?

Assignment:

1. Over the next seven days, begin and end each day by reading Numbers 6:24-26. If you are able, commit it to memory, and say it from memory at the beginning and end of each day.

2. At the next meal you share with others, pray the Jewish prayer of blessing to bless God for the meal before you. Most of all, be careful to see the meal as God's way of bowing low to bless you and allow yourself to receive His favor in it. Share with the others the difference this makes for you to see all of God's blessings this way.

CHAPTER 2

What it Means to Bless God

When God blesses us, we are moved to bless Him in return. But what does this mean? After all, isn't God self-sufficient? Doesn't He have everything He needs? What could we possibly give Him that He doesn't have already? And how could we do anything that would make any difference in the eternal, unchanging God?

I remember a time when I was struggling with these very questions, and to be specific, I was struggling to understand a particular passage of Scripture. In Ps. 103:1-2 we read:

Bless the LORD, O my soul;
   all that is within me, bless His holy name.

Bless the LORD, O my soul,
   and do not forget all His kind deeds.

I understood how God could bless us, but I couldn't understand how I—or anyone else for that matter—could possibly bless God. I was so confused, I actually prayed God would help me understand this somehow.

This was when our first child was getting close to two years of age, and more and more he was imitating the things I said and did. When I rolled a ball to him, he would roll it back. When I said simple things, he would repeat them. One of the things I would say was: "I love you Blake," and he would say, "I lu ju…."

Then, one night after a full evening of play, I carried him to his room, and just before I put him in his crib, he said, "I lu ju daddy." I literally stopped right where I was. It's hard to convey how those words made me feel except to say they blessed me. His words were completely unprompted by anything I said, and they went directly into my inner person in a way I had not experienced before. I had the immediate sense that God was answering my prayer. It was as if He was saying: "And you wanted to know how you bless Me?"

There is actually something God will never have unless we give it to Him. He will never have our hearts, but this is precisely what blesses Him. Just as we are blessed by our experience of God's heart, He is deeply blessed by His experience of ours.

Just as we are blessed by our experience of God's heart, He is deeply blessed by His experience of ours.

One reason we may struggle with the idea that we can bless God is because we tend to think that a blessing comes from unmerited favor alone. However, as we saw in the last chapter, favor can be merited or unmerited. God's unmerited favor is what moves us to live in a way that merits His favor. And there is another dynamic to this. The unmerited favor we receive from God is what moves us to merit (value) Him so highly.

In no way is the favor we show God unmerited by Him. The favor we show Him is completely merited by Him because of the unmerited favor He shows us.

I'm grateful for the way God helped me understand what it means to bless Him—and not just to understand but actually experience it. Even to this day, I continue to be moved by it. And there is actually something else in Ps. 103:1 that I didn't understand for a long time. Have you ever asked yourself why so many verses in the Bible speak of blessing God's name—as opposed to simply blessing Him? When we understand this, we are moved all the more to bless Him with all that is within us.

The Significance of a Name.

There are two things that are significant about any person's name, including God's name. To begin with, it conveys **identity**. The Israelites lived in the midst of nations that worshiped various "gods." Therefore, it was necessary for God to reveal the name by which He would be known, and the name He chose is Yahweh, which means, "I AM" (Ex. 3:13-14).

When the people blessed God's name, they were blessing Him and Him alone, and this moved in the other direction too. When they experienced God's blessings, it was because they realized the blessings came from the one true God. One of the beautiful things about the name God chose is that He was able to add certain terms to His name to describe all that He would be for His people. To give just a few examples, He is:

Yahweh Jireh: I AM your Provider (Gen. 22:14).

Yahweh Rapha: I AM your Healer (Ex. 15:26).

Yahweh Shalom: I AM your Peace (Judges 6:24).

Not only is He the self-existent One, the God who was, is, and always will be, He is the God who was, is, and always will be all we need Him to be.

Second, a name conveys **nature**. Over time, a person's name comes to be associated with certain characteristics in that person. If someone says, "I am going to fight for my name," the name has moved from mere identity to what it represents: the nature or character of the person.

Not only were the people moved to bless God's name because He is the One true God, they blessed Him also because of the nature He possessed. What then were the characteristics the people say in God's nature?

Again, we must go back to creation. When God's people looked at His creation, not only did they see the One who bowed low to bless them, they saw certain qualities in Him. In Rom. 1:20 we read:

> *When God's people looked at His creation, not only did they see the One who bowed low to bless them, they saw certain qualities in Him.*

For since the creation of the world God's invisible qualities, His eternal power and divine nature, have been clearly seen, being understood from His workmanship, so that men are without excuse.

According to this verse, God's "eternal power and divine nature" are so clear to us in creation, we have no excuse for not seeing them. What is meant though by the expression "divine nature"?

Interestingly, in the Old Testament, there are two qualities that are paired together more than any others to speak of God's nature. They are emeth (eh'-meth), which means "truth," and checed (kheh'-sed), which means "love." For example, in Ps. 85:10 we read:

Unfailing love (checed) and truth (emeth) have met
together. Righteousness and peace have kissed! NLT

Clearly, the reason these qualities are paired together so often is because they represent the two sides of God's nature we struggle so much to hold together. Our problem is that we so easily miss one side in the pursuit of the other. We miss truth in the pursuit of love, or we miss love in the pursuit of truth. However, God holds both together in perfect unison.

For this reason, based on the language of Scripture itself, I have come to believe that these qualities, truth and love, along with power constitute God's three primary characteristics, which we can also call His attributes.[4]

Power

Truth   Love

And I need to explain what I mean by "primary." In no way could we list all of God's attributes. However, these are primary in the sense that His other attributes are derived from these three—or some combination of them. To use an analogy, as it pertains to light, all the colors in the entire spectrum of colors are derived from just three colors: blue, red, and green.[5] In a similar way, we can see all of God's attributes as flowing from His power, truth, and love.

For example, out of His truth flow such attributes as justice, right-eousness, holiness, etc. From His love come mercy, grace, patience,

---

[4] Another passage that speaks of both God's power and His divine nature is 1 Pet. 1:3-4.

[5] As it pertains to material things (paint, ink, etc.), the three primary colors are red, blue, and yellow.

compassion and so forth. Out of His power come all of His unlimited capabilities, including His omniscience (all-knowing) and omnipresence (present everywhere), as well as omnipotence (all-powerful). And many of God's attributes flow out of a combination of these qualities. For example, God's goodness and faithfulness include aspects of both truth and love.

In the Bible, the word "glory" is used for the fullness of all of God's attributes combined together. To carry the previous analogy forward, when all colors contained in light are combined together, the result is what is called "white light." This is why a ray of light can be refracted into such beautiful colors when it passes through a glass prism.

If we were to assign one of the three primary colors (blue, red, or green) to each of the attributes in the diagram above, the result (represented by the intersection of all three) would be pure white. Therefore, we could say that all of God's attributes, when joined together, produces the pure white light of His glory:

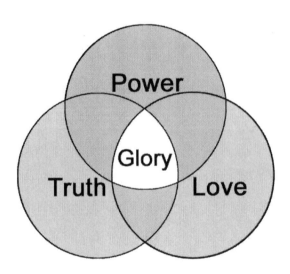

Many passages speak of the glory of God we are able to see in His creation. For example, in Ps. 19:1-3 we read:

The heavens declare the glory of God;
  the skies proclaim the work of His hands.

Day to day pours forth speech,
  And night to night reveals knowledge.

There is no speech, nor are there words;
  Their voice is not heard.

The heavens speak without words, declaring what God's glory (nature) is like.[6]

This glory of God is something we are able to see in creation as a whole. Only God could create something out of nothing. This speaks of His **power**. And in nature we see natural laws that are entirely consistent and unchanging. This speaks of His **truth**. Also, our very lives are sustained by His creation, which speaks of his **love**.

And we see these same attributes in the individual aspects of His creation as well. According to Num. 14:21, "the whole earth is filled with the glory of the LORD." And the glory of God we see in creation moves us to bless Him. In Ps. 72:18-19 we read:

Blessed be the LORD God, the God of Israel,
  who alone does marvelous deeds.

And blessed be His glorious name forever;
  all the earth be filled with His glory....

How beautiful it is to see in creation, not just the God who bowed before us, but His actual attributes—and to see them in the various aspects of His creation, including the things we take most for granted:

---

[6] In 1 Cor. 15:40-4, the word "glory" refers to the *nature* of various entities: the sun, moon, stars and various earthly bodies.

the air by which we breathe, the light by which we see, the sounds by which we hear, and on and on. And as we see His glory in creation, how good it is for us to bless Him in return for the glory He reveals, and to learn to do this more and more.

So far, we have identified two ways a name is significant. First, it conveys identity, and second, it conveys nature. If we wonder why so many Psalms speak of blessing God's name, it's because to praise His name is to praise Him and Him alone (identity), and it is to praise Him for everything His name represents (nature).

And there is still another significance of a name—at least in some cases. A name can convey **possession**. We put our name on the things we own, and this is actually what God was expressing in the blessing He instructed the priests to speak over the people of Israel. In Num. 6:27, which comes immediately after the Priestly Blessing, we read:

So they [the priests] shall put My name on the Israelites, and I will bless them. Numbers 6:27

The blessing the priests spoke over the Israelites would put God's name on them, but what does this mean?

One of the things we can't help but notice in the Priestly Blessing is how each expression begins with the words: "May the LORD…":

May the LORD bless you
    and keep you;

may the LORD cause His face to shine upon you
    and be gracious to you;

may the LORD lift up His countenance toward you
    and give you peace. Numbers 6:24-26

When we see the word "LORD" in all capitals in the Old Testament, it translates God's name, Yahweh. Therefore, as the priests spoke the words of the blessing over the people, they were placing God's name on them, and this conveyed possession. It's similar to what God spoke in Ex. 6:7: "And they will be My people, and I will be their God." It's important to see that this possession goes both ways: the people of Israel would be His people, and He would be their God. We might think of a bride who takes the name of her husband or an adoptive child who takes the name of a new mother and father.

The people were reminded that they were God's **possession** every time the priests spoke God's blessing over them, and this meant all the more to them when they realized that He was the one true God (**identity**) who possessed all power, truth, and love (**nature**):

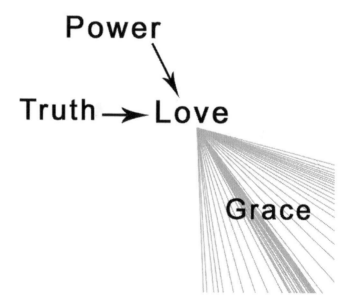

They experienced God's love in the light of His power. He is the God who created all the stars in the universe, and we know much more about this than they did. There are some billion stars in our galaxy alone and some trillion galaxies in the known universe—and the eternal God had to bow low to create them all. This is the same God who cares about every detail of our lives and bows low before us every time He blesses us.

And they experienced God's love in the light of His truth. Even though He is the God of perfect truth and righteousness, He loved them in their unrighteous condition.

This is how the experienced God's overwhelming grace toward them. As we saw in the last chapter, the expression of God's grace (chanan) consists of His compassion for the helpless and the mercy He shows to those who don't deserve it, and this is precisely what the people experienced from the God who loved them in the light of His power and truth.

How moving it was for the people to experience God's heart for them in the blessing the priests spoke over them, and this is not to say they experienced it automatically. They had to join their faith to the words spoken over them. When they did though, their sense of God's favor was unspeakable. It was like the perfect white light of His glory, shining out from His countenance on them.

There is more though.

Going back to Num. 6:27, we read: "So they shall put My name on the Israelites, and I will bless them." The last thing God speaks in the context of the Priestly Blessing is: "... and I will bless them."

Why does He emphasize this still again? Clearly, God wanted the people to experience His blessing in the words spoken over them (Num. 6:22-23), but because they were His possession, He wanted them to know He would continue to bless them with one blessing after another. God is not like the man who lavishes one gift after another on the woman he loves—until they get married.... He is just the opposite. After He placed His name on them, He would continue to bless them, and this was precisely because they had become His possession.

And because He is the God of all power, truth, and love, He was able to bless them in ways that were far more than anything they could accomplish or deserve, and this would produce in them a response that was more than they could contain. They could only bow before Him in deepest gratitude and praise.

This helps us, now, to understand the actual reason God blessed them—and the reason He blesses us.

The Reason God Blesses Us

If God's blessing moves us to bless Him, does this not point to His very purpose for blessing us? Is it not to move us to bless Him in return?

This is not to say He needs our blessing, but He is greatly blessed by it, and when we bless Him this way, a beautiful thing happens. We grow to live more and more in a relationship of mutual blessing with Him, which is His ultimate reason for blessing us:

God blesses us to draw us into a relationship of mutual blessing with Himself.

This is why it is not enough for us to receive God's blessing alone. Our blessing will never be complete until we fulfill His purpose for blessing us, which is to bless Him in return.

> *Our blessing will never be complete until we fulfill His purpose for blessing us, which is to bless Him in return.*

One evening, my wife showed me a picture a friend sent of her five-year-old daughter. She took the picture just after they arrived home late one evening. That night the stars seemed especially bright, and when her daughter saw them, she ran a short distance from their vehicle, knelt down on one knee, and began to pray.

When her mom saw this, she came closer. Her daughter's hands were clasped together, and she was praying out loud. There were no requests for anything—only prayers of thanks. This is what moved the mom to take the picture she sent my wife. When I saw it, I thought about the words of Ps. 8:3-4:

When I behold Your heavens,
　　The work of Your fingers,

The moon and the stars,
　　Which You have set in place—

What is man that You are mindful of him,
　　Or the son of man that You care for him?

Interestingly, here is the verse that comes just before these verses:

From the mouths of children and infants
　　You have ordained praise…. Psalm 8:2

As I continued to look at this picture, I couldn't help but think about how this little child's prayers must have blessed the God of heaven. I felt like I was looking into eternity past and seeing what moved the heart of the eternal God to bring forth all of creation, including our lives. He longed for us to experience the greatness of His love, but He also longed to experience our love in return.

And I was also moved to think how blessed this little girl must have been to possess such a heart of praise for the God of heaven. There are some who merely walk beneath the stars, and there are others who bow down before the God who created them, and we don't have to wonder which are most blessed.

Even as you read these words, you may be thinking: "The heart of this little girl is something I long for, but there is no way I could ever possess that kind of heart. The innocence of that child is something I lost a long time ago, and there is no way the God of heaven could ever love the heart I now possess."

If that is how you feel, may I assure you that you can possess that kind of heart again? And the reason is because, as we will see in the next chapter, when the eternal God bowed low to bring forth the heavens and the earth,

it wasn't the last time He would bow before His entire creation....

Summary

- Just as we are blessed by our experience of God's heart, He is blessed by His experience of ours.
- The unmerited favor God shows us moves us to praise and thank God for the favor He completely merits from us.
- Names are significant because they convey identity, nature, and possession.
- The two attributes that are paired together more than any others to speak of God's nature in the Old Testament are:

  emeth = truth

  checed = love

- Three primary characteristics of God nature are power, truth, and love.
- The word used for the fullness of God's nature (the combination of all His attributes) is "glory".
- The reason God blesses us is to draw us into a relationship of mutual blessing with Himself.

Discussion Questions
For Chapter 2

1. Are there specific ways God spoke to you through this chapter?

2. What are three ways a name is significant? Explain what is meant by each of these.

3. Why do so many passages of Scripture speak of praising God's name—as opposed to praising Him?

4. What two attributes of God are paired together more than any others in the Old Testament? Why are these two attributes paired together so often to speak of God's nature?

5. What were the three primary attributes of God that were given in this chapter? What is meant by "primary"?

6. What are some specific aspects of God's creation that move you to see His glory? How can you see His power, truth, and love in each of these?

7. In your own words, why does God bless us?

Assignment:

1. Memorize Ps. 103:1-2.

2. Sometime during the next seven days, find a place to go on a "nature walk" (whether alone or with a friend) and let your goal be to see His nature. As you walk, look for aspects of God's creation that reveal His glory. Think about how each one reveals His power, truth, and love. Let your heart be moved to bless Him with your praise and thanksgiving for all the glory you see.

CHAPTER 3

The Blessing of Grace

On the evening before Jesus went to the cross, He gave His disciples a very powerful object lesson. During the last meal that He would share with them before His suffering, He rose from the table, took a bowl of water and a towel in hand, and began to wash their feet. Of course, this is not what any of them would have expected. In that day, the task of washing feet belonged to the servant in the home. This is why Peter protested so strongly: "Never shall you wash my feet!" Jesus answered by saying: "Unless I wash you, you have no part with Me (John 13:8)."

What did Jesus mean by this? Clearly, He was communicating His very purpose for entering the world. On the very next day He would give His life as a sacrifice for the sins of the world. This is how He came to "wash" us, and this is the very essence of the gospel (good news). Our natural inclination is to think our salvation comes from what we do for God, but it comes only from what we allow Him to do for us.

When I was in college, a very generous individual made a way for me to travel to Israel with a small group. We stayed at the Ramada Shalom. (What a great name for a hotel....) One day, as I was walking up one of the stairwells, I met a custodian. He was very kind and seemed intrigued to learn more about this visitor from the U.S. I learned he was Muslim by birth, and somehow our conversation turned to what is necessary for a person to go to heaven. As we sat on the stairs, he shared with me his understanding. He said I should draw a line down the center of a piece of paper. Then I should write all the good things I have done on one side of the line and all the bad things on the other side. And if the good things outnumbered the bad, I would get in.

I then shared with Him my understanding. I told him that none of us can make it into heaven with even one mark against us, and this is because God is utterly holy, and He can't have fellowship with that which is unholy. I explained that this is the reason Jesus died for us. By His sacrifice He paid the penalty for our sins, and when we put our trust in His sacrifice for us, He forgives us completely. It's as if He tears up the entire list of the bad things we have done, and this is what enables us to enter His presence.

I remember the look on his face as I shared these things. He seemed very glad—and even relieved—to hear what I said. Later that day he went out of his way to find me, and when he did, he gave me an apple with a knife in it. It was his way of thanking me.

And yes, I was glad the knife was for the apple and not some other purpose....

I also remembered Jesus' words in Matt. 10:42, that whoever gives even a cup of cold water to one of His disciples will never lose his reward. Since that day I have found myself praying often that Jesus' promise applies to apples as well as water.

In Eph. 2:8-9 the apostle Paul writes:

For it is by grace you have been saved through faith, and this not from yourselves; it is the gift of God, not by works, so that no one can boast.

The word "grace" in these verses comes from the Greek word *charis* (khar'-ese), which means "favor." As we have seen, there are two primary words for favor in the Old Testament: *chanan* (unmerited favor) and *ratsah* (merited favor). In the New Testament, this one word, *charis*, is used for both, and the context determines which one it refers to. In this passage, it clearly refers to unmerited favor. Our salvation is "the gift of God." It is not something we can earn by our works. We receive this gift only by trusting in Him, by faith, to do for us what we can't do for ourselves.

When Peter learned he could have no part with Jesus unless he let Jesus wash him, he said: "Then, Lord, not only my feet, but my hands and my head as well (John 13:9)!" Jesus responded this time in a way we might not have expected: "Whoever has already bathed needs only to wash his feet, and he will be completely clean (John 13:10)."

Peter was already "clean" because he had placed his faith in Jesus (Matt. 16:16). However, as long as he lived in this world, he would pick up the "dirt" of this world—just as we all do. As the apostle James writes, "We all stumble in many ways… (Jas. 3:2)," and this is why we have to keep coming back to let Him wash us over and over again.

Three Aspects of Salvation

Unfortunately, our concept of salvation can be very shallow. In Scripture, there are three very distinct aspects of salvation, and it's essential for us to understand each one.

Justification

The first aspect of salvation is "justification." In Rom. 5:1, the apostle Paul writes:

> Therefore, since we have been justified through faith, we have peace with God through our Lord Jesus Christ.

To be justified is to be made righteous (just) in God's sight, even though we are not righteous in and of ourselves. This is made possible only by Jesus' sacrifice for us. Not only is God a God of perfect love and mercy, He also possesses perfect truth and justice. Therefore, a just penalty was required for our sins. However, rather than placing on us the penalty we deserved, He allowed it to fall on His own Son. This is how He demonstrated His love for us (Rom. 5:8), and it's how He was able to remain just while justifying us, as we read in Rom. 3:26: "... so as to be just and the justifier of the one who has faith in Jesus."

In 2 Cor. 5:21, we read:

> God made Him who knew no sin to be sin on our behalf, so that in Him we might become the righteousness of God.

When we trust in Jesus' sacrifice for us, the *Great Exchange* takes place. All of our sin is placed on Him, and all of His righteousness is placed on us, and when we do this, as hard as this may be for us to comprehend—or even accept, God sees us as being as holy and as righteous as His Son Jesus.

> *When we trust in Jesus' sacrifice for us, the Great Exchange takes place. All of our sin is placed on Him, and all of His righteousness is placed on us*

Sanctification

The second aspect of salvation is sanctification. In 1 Thess. 5:23 we read:

Now may the God of peace Himself sanctify you completely, and may your entire spirit, soul, and body be kept blameless at the coming of our Lord Jesus Christ.

To "sanctify" means to "make holy," and this is a process. When we first trust in Jesus, God makes us righteous in our *position* before Him (justification). Then He works to make us more and more righteous in our actual *experience* (how we live) before Him (sanctification). This begins when we first trust in Him, but it will not be complete until we go to be with Him in heaven one day.

As we see in the verse above, God wants to sanctify us in the totality of our lives: spirit, soul, and body. We are unique in that God created us to possess all three. Plant life has a living body, but no soul. Animals have a living body and soul, which consists of the mind, will, and emotions—that which "animates" the body. However, we possess body, soul, and spirit. Our spirit is what gives us the capacity for a relationship with God, who is spirit (John 4:24).

Here, the apostle Paul prays that God will sanctify us in every part of our beings. First, when we put our trust in Jesus' sacrifice for us, *our spirits* are born of His Spirit (John 3:1-8). Then, as God's Spirit lives in us, He works to make us more and more like Him in *our souls*. This process actually affects the way we live in *our bodies*, and this will continue until we receive completely new bodies one day.

Glorification

The third aspect of salvation is glorification. In Phil. 3:20-21, Paul writes:

But our citizenship is in heaven, and we eagerly await a Savior from there, the Lord Jesus Christ, who, by the power that enables Him to subject all things to Himself, will transform our lowly bodies to be like His glorious body.

Jesus' "glorious body" is the kind of body we will possess in heaven one day. As we have seen, the word "glory" refers to one's nature. In heaven, our bodies will possess an entirely new nature that is fit for eternity. This is what the apostle Paul was speaking of when he said our bodies will be "raised in glory" (1 Cor. 15:43). When that happens, Paul continues: "… the perishable must be clothed with the imperishable, and the mortal with immortality (1 Cor. 15:53)."

And this new *nature* includes our entire beings: spirit, soul, and body. Our bodies will be completely new, and our souls will no longer wage the battle between our spirit and flesh (Matt. 26:41), and our spirits will be completely free from the bondage of sin we experience in our souls our bodies. Glory!

In heaven we will be "like" Jesus (1 John 3:2), and this does not mean we will share in His deity, but we will share in His righteousness. In this sense, our nature will be like His.

By way of summary, in justification God makes us righteous in our position before Him. Then, in sanctification, He makes us more and more righteous in our experience before Him. And in glorification, He makes us completely righteous in our nature before Him.

And there are other ways we can describe these three aspects of salvation. First, He saves us from **the penalty of sin**. Then He saves us more and more from **the power of sin**, and one day He will save us from the **very presence of sin**.

And here is still another way. First, He saves us **in our spirits**. Then, He works to save us more and more **in our souls**. And one day he will save us **in our bodies**.

The important thing for us to understand is that each aspect of salvation is the work of His grace. By grace we **are saved, continue to be saved,** and **will be saved**.

Three Aspects of Salvation

Justification	Sanctification	Glorification
Righteous in Our Position Before God	Righteous in Our Experience Before God	Righteous in Our Nature Before God
Saved from the Penalty of Sin	Saved from the Power of Sin	Saved from the Presence of Sin
Saved in our Spirits	Saved in our Souls	Saved in our Bodies
Grace by which We Are Saved	Grace by which We Continue to be Saved	Grace by which We Will be Saved

This gives us a more complete picture of salvation as we see it in Scripture, but it brings up a question. How can grace make us righteous in our actual experience before God? After all, if we know God is willing to forgive us over and over again, wouldn't that make us more likely to sin?

It may appear that way—until we experience true grace.

The Power of Grace

When we taste true grace, we never see it as an excuse to sin. Just the opposite, we discover a new power to overcome our sins, and there are multiple reasons for this.

Grace Heals Us. As we have seen, our peace comes from righteousness, which we can understand as "right alignment." This begins with our alignment with God, which reveals also the source of our lack of peace, which is our lack of alignment with Him, and this carries over to our relationship with the world and those we share the world with.

Our tendency is to try to fix this problem. However, the solution begins with what we allow God to do for us. We must trust in His grace alone, by faith alone. When we do this, He rightly aligns our lives by His gift. Then, He moves us, by His grace to align our lives more and more, not out of obligation or burden, but out of gratitude for what He has done for us.

This is a process though. Our old habits and thought patterns can be hard to overcome. There are many who were raised in graceless homes. They were taught that their worth depended on their accomplishments, and they never learned of the worth they possess simply because they are God's creation. In their minds, it's as if they are listening to music, but it's not good music. It tells them, "No matter what you do, you will never measure up, and it will never be enough...." They don't realize the music is playing though, because they have never known anything different. What they need to hear is "new music."

I love the words of Zeph. 3:17:

The LORD your God is among you;
    He is mighty to save.

He will rejoice over you with gladness;
    He will quiet you with His love;
    He will rejoice over you with singing.

This is the "music" of grace. God accepts us and is for us and delights in us. It is music that aligns our lives with God and gives us peace. This music quite literally "saves our souls." It rescues our mind, will, and emotions, and the more we hear this music of grace, the more healing we find. This also carries over to every aspect of our lives, bringing us into more and more alignment, which brings us more and more peace.

Grace Satisfies Us. Not only does grace heal, it satisfies. Why is it that we "look for love in all the wrong places?" Isn't it because we are trying to satisfy our souls in ways that can never really satisfy us? When we know true grace though, we experience the satisfaction God brings to our inner person.

Then, when we have known this peace, we can't be satisfied with anything less. When we stumble in some way, we want confess our sins, so we can return to the closeness of our fellowship with God and experience His peace again.

And something else happens. Because we find satisfaction in the grace He pours into us, we don't need to seek it in the things that never could satisfy us, and we begin to find true satisfaction in good gifts God gives, because we are now able to receive them in peace and contentment.

In all these ways, grace has a refining, purifying effect on our lives.

Years ago, I taught at a Vacation Bible School for young children, and my assignment one day was to teach on the topic of sin. After listening to me teach on the dangers of sin, a young boy raised his hand and asked, "But if we're not supposed to sin, how can we have any fun?" It was hard to keep the smile from breaking out on my face, and the thing that made his question so funny to me was the look of utter sincerity on his face. He was truly conflicted.

The lies we believe begin early don't they?

The true righteousness of right alignment is not the judgmental, self-righteous, mean spirited, legalistic, empty religion that some people see it as. Those are actually the things produced by a life devoid of grace and the inability to show it.

True righteousness is the most winsome, attractive, balanced, healthy, grounded, joyful, free and *satisfying* life we can live. These are the things grace produces in the soul of the One who receives it, because these are the things that belong to the nature of the God who gives it.

Grace Moves Us. We are all motivated in multiple ways. To begin with, we are motivated by the fear of loss and the promise of gain. Both are completely valid. Parents use them. Teachers and coaches us them. Even God uses them. However, there is a far greater motivator than either of these.

To illustrate, athletes who perform very high levels are certainly motivated by the fear of loss and the promise of gain, but many are fueled by an even greater motivation. It may come from a mother who worked multiple jobs to put food on the table or a father who never gave up on them. This is the motivation of *grace*. It is birthed, not in what can be gained, but in what has already been given. Blessed are children who receive this kind of motivation. It produces in them a passion like no other. And blessed are we when we realize this is the motivation we already possess in Christ.

> *This is the motivation of grace. It is birthed, not in what can be gained, but in what has already been given.*

I'm always moved by the picture of Mary (the sister of Lazarus), who washed Jesus' feet with expensive perfume, and then dried His feet with her hair (Luke 12:1-8). What moved her to do this? Was it fear of punishment? Not at all. Was it the promise of a reward? No. It was grace alone. Grace is the most altruistic motivation we can have because it is not focused on self-interest at all. It is overwhelmed with the interest of the One who has shown us such kindness. This is why it is the most beautiful, powerful, freeing, and glorious motivation of all.

How does grace make us more and more righteous in our actual *experience*? It heals our past, satisfies our present, and moves us into an entirely new future.

And there is no greater example of this than Peter himself.

On the night Jesus washed Peter's feet, Peter promised to lay down his life for Jesus (John 13:37), and he even boasted he would never fall away—even if everyone else did (Matt. 26:33). Jesus knew, however, what Peter would do before the sun rose the next day. Peter would deny Him three times. Jesus spoke this to him ahead of time (Matt. 26:34), and this is precisely what happened. In Matt. 26:75, we find one of the most poignant verses of in all of Scripture. When Peter heard the rooster's crow the following morning, he went out and "wept bitterly."

After His resurrection, Jesus told His disciples to wait for Him in the region of Galilee. Can you imagine how Peter must have felt as he waited? Jesus had called him to be a fisher of men. However, was all of this off now? Was this the reason Peter decided to go fishing when he reached Galilee—for fish (John 21:1-3)?

When Jesus finally spoke to Peter, He asked him three times if he loved Him. This gave Peter a chance to reaffirm his love for Jesus three times, once for each time he denied Him, and each time Peter reaffirmed his love for Jesus, Jesus reaffirmed His call to Peter to care for His sheep. Surely there was no greater way for Jesus to express His love for Peter. He still believed in Him.

Earlier, when Jesus first washed Peter's feet, he told him that he would not understand what He was doing until later (John 11:7). Was this when Peter understood? Not only did he need Jesus to wash him at the beginning; he needed Jesus to continue to wash him always. This is when Peter learned that Jesus didn't just love him at the start; He loved him *still*.

From this moment Peter would be a very different person. The boasting in himself gave way to boasting in His Savior, and the letters he would write (1 and 2 Peter) would be filled with grace. What then can we learn from His example?

To begin with, we must rely completely on the God's grace for our right standing before Him. With this in mind, here is a question we would all do well to ask ourselves, because our answer reveals so much. Are you able to say:

I see myself as being as holy and righteous in the sight of God as the Lord Jesus Christ.

If you are not able to say this, it is because you are still not relying completely on His grace alone.

I have to say there are days when I still struggle to believe God could see me this way. Perhaps it's because I understand how He could forgive me at the start, but I struggle to believe He could forgive me even after I should have known better.

There is something I find great help in though in the words of Peter (yes, Peter). In his second letter in our New Testament, he gives us the qualities we need in order to grow in our knowledge of the Lord Jesus Christ (2 Pet. 1:5-8). Then he tells us what the cause is if we don't have these qualities:

But whoever lacks these traits is nearsighted to the point of blindness, having forgotten that he has been cleansed from his past sins. 2 Peter 2:9.

It's interesting to see what Peter does *not* say. He doesn't say the problem is that we aren't trying hard enough. He doesn't give us a new list of things that we must do. He says we have "forgotten" that we have been cleansed. Why? The same grace we rely on at the beginning is the grace we must rely on always. And if we will do this, it will produce in us the ongoing effect it had at the

> The same grace we rely on at the beginning is the grace we must rely on always.

beginning. His grace will become for us a continual supply of healing, satisfaction, and motivation—all the things that help us grow in true righteousness.

Here is the great irony. If we push away grace because we believe we are not worthy of it, we push away the only thing that can make us worthy, and we push away the only thing that can move us to live a life that is worthy of the grace we have been given.

What then must we do? We must rely on His righteousness alone.

In Luke 18:10-14, we see the parable Jesus spoke to those "who trusted in their own righteousness and viewed others with contempt" (Luke 18:9):

> Two men went up to the temple to pray. One was a Pharisee and the other a tax collector. The Pharisee stood by himself and prayed, "God, I thank You that I am not like the other men— swindlers, evildoers, adulterers—or even like this tax collector. I fast twice a week and pay tithes of all that I acquire."
>
> But the tax collector stood at a distance, unwilling even to lift up his eyes to heaven. Instead, he beat his breast and said, "God, have mercy on me, a sinner!" I tell you, this man, rather than the Pharisee, went home justified. For everyone who ex- alts himself will be humbled, but the one who humbles himself will be exalted. (Luke 18:10-14)

In that day, the Pharisees were highly regarded because they were determined (at least outwardly) to keep every detail of the law. And tax collectors were among the most despised, because they collected taxes on behalf of their Roman occupiers. However, Jesus said that one of the two went home "justified." It wasn't the one who believed he was righteous. It was the one who cried out to the living God for a righteousness he knew he didn't possess.

> *If it was enough for a humble tax collector, it's enough for us. We must say: "Be merciful to me a sinner."*

What then must we do? If it was enough for a humble tax collector, it's enough for us. We must say: "Be merciful to me a sinner."

How could this ever be even possible for us though? It's possible because the God who bowed low to create the heavens and the earth did not leave us to ourselves. Out of His great love He entered our world to bow again, this time to take away our sins, and to rescue us for Himself. He did it to keep us, to be gracious to us, and to give us His peace.

This is what Jesus was picturing when He washed the feet of His disciples on the night before His sacrifice, and the same One who bowed before them is the who stands ready to bow before each of us.

Can you see Him? He has a bowl of water and a towel in His hands. Will you let Him wash you now?

Will you let Him wash you always?

Summary

- The New Testament word for grace is *charis*, which refers to favor that can be merited or unmerited, and the context determines which one it refers to.

- We are saved by grace (unmerited favor) through faith (Eph. 2:8-9). It is the gift of God, so we can't boast that we have earned it.
- There are three aspects of salvation: **Justification** is the means by which we are made righteous in our position before God. **Sanctification** is the means by which we are made righteous in our experience before God. **Glorification** is the means by which we will be made righteous in our very nature before God.
- Every aspect of salvation is accomplished in us by grace. By grace we are saved, continue to be saved, and will be saved.
- Grace accomplishes the work of sanctification in us by healing us, satisfying us, and moving (motivating) us.
- If we are not able to see ourselves as being as holy and righteous as the Lord Jesus Christ, we are still not relying fully on grace.
- Just as we must rely on the grace of God to save us at the beginning, we must rely on His grace always.
- When we rely on grace for the gift of righteousness, we are moved to live lives that are worthy of God's grace, not because we are working to receive it, but because we have already received it.

Discussion Questions
for Chapter 3

1. Are there specific ways God spoke to you through this chapter?

2. What are the three aspects of salvation? What is meant by each one?

3. What would you say to someone who says: "Doesn't grace give us all an excuse to sin?"

4. How does grace give us power to overcome sin?

5. Do you ever feel like you are listening to "the wrong music" in your mind? If so, what can you do to overcome it?

6. Why can it be good if we feel unworthy of God's forgiveness? What is necessary for us to receive God's forgiveness?

7. Are you able to say: "I am as holy and righteous in the sight of God as the Lord Jesus Christ"? If so, give thanks to God for His grace. If not, what keeps you from saying this? Share this with those who will pray for you and help you receive and live in the true grace of God.

Assignment:

1. Memorize these two verses: Eph. 2:8-9. 1 John 1:9.

2. Over the next seven days, remember that "the Great Exchange" has taken place if you have put your trust in the Lord Jesus Christ for salvation. Then, be careful to come back to Jesus for His forgiveness as often as you need to.

CHAPTER 4

Our Greatest Blessing

One day, as Jesus and His disciples were traveling from Judea to Galilee, they came to a town called Sychar in the region of Samaria. Because Jesus was weary from the journey, He sat down next to a well. After His disciples went into town to buy food, a woman came to that same well to draw water. When she arrived, Jesus asked her for a drink. This surprised her because she was a Samaritan. In those days, the Jews had no association with Samaritans, so she asked Him how He, being a Jew, could ask her for a drink. Jesus replied by saying:

> If you knew the gift of God and who is asking you for a drink, you would have asked Him, and He would have given you living water. (John 4:10)

What was this "living water" Jesus spoke of? We see the answer just a few chapters later. In John 7:38, Jesus says:

> Whoever believes in Me, as the Scripture has said: "Streams of living water will flow from within him."

Then, in the following verse, we read:

He was speaking about the Spirit, whom those who believed in Him were later to receive…. (John 7:39)

The living water Jesus spoke of is the Holy Spirit.

And there is something else we need to be clear about. What was the "the gift of God" Jesus spoke of in John 4:10? We might think it was the living water. However, the gift of God and the One asking for a drink are one in the same. Therefore, "the gift of God" was none other than Jesus Himself.[7]

Why is it so important for us to be clear about this? It's because Jesus is not "a gift"; He is "the gift." That is, He is God's ultimate and greatest gift to us, and this makes Him our very greatest blessing too.

Going back to our definition for "a blessing," where should we see Jesus in the definition?

A blessing is a gift God gives as an expression of His favor.

And because Jesus is our greatest blessing, we can expand on this definition by saying:

Our greatest blessing is Jesus, the Father's greatest gift to us and the highest expression of His favor.

It's vitally important for us to see Jesus this way—as the greatest gift and blessing of God, because when we do, we see many things as we should, beginning with Jesus Himself.

---

[7] Jesus said, "If you knew the gift of God…., you would have asked…." Therefore, if the gift of God was the living water, she would not need to ask for it, having known it already." Also, in John 4:14, Jesus is the One who gives the living water. If "the gift of God" in John 4:10 referred to the living water, we should see it as coming from Him (God the Father). Jesus was both the gift of God *and* the One speaking to her, and if she would ask Him (Jesus), then He would give her this living water.

When we See the Gift of God as we Should, we See:

Jesus as we Should

In John 1:14 we read:

The Word became flesh and made His dwelling among us. We have seen His glory, the glory of the one and only Son from the Father, full of grace and truth.

The "Word" John speaks of here is Jesus. He is the One who became flesh and made His dwelling among us. And John is describing His glory was like. As we have seen, one's glory is one's nature. Therefore, John is describing what He and the other disciples observed in Jesus' nature. He was "full of grace and truth." And there is a reason He possessed this nature. It's because He was the one and only Son from the Father.

As we have seen, the two attributes of God that are paired together more than any others in the Old Testament are truth and love. Therefore, it shouldn't surprise us that Jesus' nature would be described in such a similar way. Like the Father, the Son had the power to hold together both sides of the divine nature in perfect unison. This is what Jesus' disciples saw in Him, and I'm convinced this is what this Samaritan woman saw in Jesus as well.

When Jesus offered her living water, she didn't get it at first. She said:

… You have nothing to draw with and the well is deep. Where then will You get this living water." (John 4:11)

Jesus answered:

Everyone who drinks this water will be thirsty again. But whoever drinks the water I give him will never thirst. Indeed, the water I give him will become in him a fount of water springing up to eternal life. (John 4:13-14)

When she heard this, she said: "Sir, give me this water so that I will not get thirsty and have to keep coming here to draw water (John 4:15)." Jesus told her to call her husband and come back. She said she didn't have a husband (John 4:16-17), and Jesus said:

... You are correct to say that you have no husband. In fact, you have had five husbands, and the man you now have is not your husband. You have spoken truthfully. (John 4:17-18)

Here is what I find so fascinating. As we continue to observe Jesus' interaction with this woman, we do not get the impression that she felt judged or condemned in any way. Why? It's because Jesus was full of grace and truth. Yes, He spoke truth, but she could sense that it came only in love. That's grace....

If we saw Jesus as He truly is, we would never fail to trust Him, and we would never hesitate to follow Him. He is "the gift of God." Therefore, He possesses the same nature as His Father, full of grace and truth. And ironically, when we see Jesus this way, it helps us see the Father as we should as well.

I never feel adequate to express the gift God has given us in Christ. The best way I know how to even begin is with Peter's words in 1 Pet. 1:18-19:

For you know that it was not with perishable things such as silver or gold that you were redeemed from the empty way of life you inherited from your forefathers, but with the precious blood of Christ, a lamb without blemish or spot.

The word "redeemed" here comes from the Hebrew word *lutroo* (loo-tro'-o), which means "to purchase back" or "to restore possession to the rightful owner." When it came time for God to redeem us, what price could ever be adequate to restore us to Himself? Peter says God did not redeem us with perishable things such as silver and gold. After all, what amount of silver or gold would be enough to purchase our lives for Him? We were redeemed "with the precious blood of Christ, a lamb without blemish or spot." And here is what is so important for us to understand: A price paid reveals, not just the cost incurred, but the value of what is purchased.

> A price paid reveals, not just the cost incurred, but the value of what is purchased.

What value, then, did God place on us? It was the value He placed on His own Son, and there is nothing that does more to reveal His heart for us.

There are some who see Jesus as the compassionate and kind one, but they see the Father as harsh and demanding. We would never see Him this way though if we truly understood the gift He gave us in Christ.

When we see "the gift of God" as we should, we see Jesus as we should, and we see the Father as we should, and based on Jesus' interaction with this woman, we should add something else too: we see the Holy Spirit as we should.

In John 4 we see a powerful example of the relationship between the Father, Son, and Holy Spirit. The Son is the gift of the Father, and from the Son we receive the gift of the Spirit. This relationship between the Father, Son, and Spirit is what we call "the Trinity," which means "three in one" (tri-unity). That which is triune is distinguishable but inseparable. Three (distinguishable) are one (inseparable). Therefore, the Father, Son, and Holy Spirit all possess the same glory: full of grace and truth.

I must say I have not always seen the Holy Spirit as I should. I'm sure this is, at least in part, due to my prideful resistance to His leadership, and it may also come from what I have observed in some who *claim* to live under His leadership. However, it makes no sense for me to see the nature of the Spirit as any different from that of the Father and the Son. The Holy Spirit is none other than the Spirit of Christ and of the Father (Rom. 8:9, 1 Pet. 1:11).

If we saw "the gift of God as we should," we would see the Son, the Father, and the Spirit as we should. There is a reason, though, for giving particular focus to the centrality of Jesus. He is the supreme *expression* of God's grace. Then, issuing out from Jesus, we receive the Holy Spirit, who becomes for us our greatest *experience* of God's grace, pouring into our hearts like living water.

God

Jesus

Holy Spirit

And when we see "the gift of God" as we should, there is more we see as we should....

We see Grace as we Should

Based on what we learned in the last chapter, it would be easy to conclude that grace is our greatest blessing. After all, grace is the means by which we are saved, continue to be saved, and will be saved. However, there are important reasons to emphasize that Jesus is our greatest blessing, even above the blessing of grace.

To begin with, as beautiful and powerful as grace is, it is not an end in itself; it is a means to a greater end. In the last chapter we saw Jesus' words to Peter: "Unless I wash you, you have no part with Me (John 13:8)." Therefore, Jesus' washing, which is the grace He showed, was the means to a greater

> *as beautiful and powerful as grace is, it is not an end in itself; it is a means to a greater end.*

end, which is to share in His life.

Unfortunately, it's possible to seek grace above the God who gives it. This happens when we seek the forgiveness that comes from grace, but we have no interest in knowing the One who forgives. In his classic book, "The Cost of Discipleship," Dietrich Bonhoeffer speaks out against what he calls "cheap grace."

> Cheap grace is grace without discipleship, grace without the cross, grace without Jesus Christ, living and incarnate.[8]
>
> Dietrich Bonhoeffer

If this is how we see grace, we don't know the role of grace in our lives, and we don't know the actual nature of the One who gives it. Perhaps an illustration would help to convey this.

Imagine a young girl who lives as an orphan on the streets of a large city. One evening, as night is about to fall, it's very cold outside, and she's hungry, so she does what she often does about this time each day: she walks the streets of the city in search of food. This night she travels far enough to come to a beautiful home, and as she looks through the front window, she sees children playing inside. She sees a mother and father, something she has never known. There is a fire in the fireplace. She can hear the sound of music coming from the house.

---

[8] Dietrich Bonhoeffer, *The Cost of Discipleship*, rev. ed. (New York: Macmillan Publishing Co. Inc., 1963), p. 47.

As she looks inside, her heart longs for a home like that. How could she ever find herself in a home like that though? Her clothes are in shambles. She hasn't bathed in weeks. Many of the meals she has survived on are meals she has stolen.

By chance that evening—or perhaps not by chance—the father looks out the window and sees her, and compassion seizes his heart. He steps outside to ask if she would like to come it and to share in their meal together. At first, it's hard for her to accept the invitation. She doesn't feel like she would fit in. However, her hunger overcomes her resistance, so she enters.

As she shares in this meal, she is overwhelmed by the kindness of this family. And the father's compassion for her only grows. After the meal, he can't release her back to the streets, so he invites her to stay the night.

The next day, out of gratitude, she helps with anything she can around the house. The father invites her to stay the entire day, and then, again, he invites her to stay through the night again. One day turns into another day and another. Then one day, after consulting with all the family, the father asks her if she would like to be a part of their family.

Going back now to the night she stood outside, looking through the window of that house, what was her greatest longing? It was to be a part of a family like the one she saw through the window. And what would be needed for that to happen? In a word, it was grace, but the grace was only the means to something greater....

The reason I share this is because some see grace as an excuse to live their lives apart from God. After all, because He is a God of grace, He will surely understand. What they don't realize is that grace, which a great thing, is only the means to the greatest thing, which is to know Him.

Grace is not the permission God gives to stay away; it's the invitation He gives to all to come in. And there is a beautiful thing that happens when we "enter in." The grace that first brought to the living

> Grace is not the permission God gives to stay away; it's the invitation He gives to all to come in.

God becomes what we receive, continually, from Him.

And secondly, not only is grace a means to the greater end of knowing Christ, it is also from Christ that grace is poured into our lives by the Holy Spirit. Continuing the analogy above, if only the little girl could accept the incredible gift so graciously offered her, then she would know the true source of the grace that was held out to her, and she would realize that a continual supply of grace and everything she needed along with it.

As glorious as grace is, its very purpose is to draw us to Christ, and from Christ we receive the ongoing experience of His grace. In each case, Christ is higher, and we must always see Him this way if we are going to know His true grace.

When we see "the gift of God" as we should, we see Jesus and grace as we should, and there is still something else we see as we should....

We See God's Blessings as We Should

As we listen in to Jesus' conversation with this woman, we get the distinct impression that there is a reason He was so eager for her to know the living water only He could give her. It's because there was a place in her soul that she was trying to satisfy with things that could never ultimately satisfy her.

We don't know everything about her, including her upbringing, the hurts she experienced, what led to her multiple marriages, why she decided to live with a man who was not her husband, etc., but the truth is that she is no different from any of us. In a sense, she is a picture of all of us, because we are trying to satisfy our "thirst," even if we are attempting to do this in different ways.

And we are all like her in another way. The solution for all of us is the same. It is the living water only Jesus can give. Only from Him can we experience the true blessing that issues forth from His grace.

As we have learned, God's blessings do not consist of the gifts He gives alone; it consists of the favor we experience in His gifts. Unfortunately, it is possible to seek the blessing apart from grace, but when we do, we miss both grace and His blessing.

And as we have seen in this chapter, it is also possible to seek grace apart from Christ, but when we do this, not only do we miss Him, we miss the grace and the blessing that comes from Him.

Jesus

Grace

Blessing

Only when we seek Him first do we experience His grace and the blessing that issues forth from it. Apart from Him we have nothing, but in Him we have everything.

This is why we need to see Him as our greatest blessing. If we don't do this, the blessings we seek will only interfere with our true blessing in Him. However, if we seek Him as our greatest blessing, then we will know ever blessing that flows from His grace.

When we know Him as our greatest blessing, in no way does this diminish our appreciation for the blessings He gives; it will only increase our appreciation for them, because we will see them as coming from Him. And it only increases our appreciation for Him, because He is the One who gives the gifts.

In Jesus' interaction with the woman at the well, there is much we learn about Jesus, "the gift of God" and our greatest blessing, and as their conversation continues, we also see much about this woman that is very moving to us.

In spite of the challenges she experienced, she appears to have been an honest person. When Jesus asked her to call her husband and come back, she said she didn't have a husband. This was very important because there was nothing in her that was beyond the reach of God's forgiveness except her ability to be honest about sin and to trust in God's grace alone. Therefore, it's good that she was honest.

Also, she appears to have been a devout woman. When Jesus revealed His knowledge about certain things He had no natural way of knowing, she perceived Him to be a prophet (John 4:19). This moved her to bring up certain questions about disputes between the Jews and Samaritans. In this she was clearly seeking truth, and in no way did Jesus minimize the importance of the truth, but He emphasized that truth alone is not enough. God in spirit. Therefore, His worshipers much worship Him in spirit and truth (John 4:24).

In this, Jesus was identifying what she needed most. Deep within her spirit, the place God created for Himself, she needed the living water of God's Spirit. This alone would satisfy her in her inner person, and this living water would spring up in her to eternal life.

It's important for us to understand what Jesus meant by "eternal life." In John 17:3 we read:

> Now this is eternal life, that they may know You, the only true God, and Jesus Christ, whom You have sent.

Here the "eternal life" refers to the Jesus and the Father possessed. This life will certainly be present in heaven, but it is also available now. The apostle John says this same thing in 1 John 5:11-12:

> And this is that testimony: God has given us eternal life, and this life is in His Son. Whoever has the Son has life; whoever does not have the Son of God does not have life.

The eternal life John speaks of here is in the Son, and whoever has the Son has that life (eternal life). Again, this life is available now, and this is the life that would spring up from this woman when she received the living water. The life of the Spirit would enter her spirit, and it would spring up to her soul and to the tangible aspects of her life. It would produce lasting satisfaction in her inner person, so she would never thirst again.

At the time, she couldn't understand everything Jesus was saying, and we can't blame her, so she simply said: "I know that Messiah is coming. When He comes, He will explain everything to us (John 4:25)." Jesus replied:

> I who speak to you am He. (John 4:26)

Talk about a "Drop the mic" moment….

Just then, Jesus' disciples returned from their trip into town for food, and John observed something a small thing, which was actually quite large thing. It's one of the most beautiful and stirring details in any narrative of Scripture. When this woman left to go tell the people of her town about the man she met, she "left the water jar" behind.

The words Jesus spoke gave birth to faith in her. Now she possessed a greater water, and she would never need to thirst again.

Based on all we have learned from Jesus' encounter with her, what then is necessary for us to know our very greatest blessing?

To Know our Greatest Blessing, we Must:

Know the Gift of God. Our focus in this chapter has been on how we see "the gift of God." However, there is something that is even more important than this. Jesus said to the woman, "If you knew the gift of God...." *We must know Him.* And we come to know Him when we believe in Him and rely fully on His grace.

Ask for Living Water. Why did Jesus ask this woman for water? Yes, He was weary and thirsty, but was there another reason? When Jesus was thirsty, what did He do? He asked for a drink. And what did she need to do to receive the living water? Just ask. What then was Jesus doing? He was modeling for her what she needed to do to receive the living water. Yes, Jesus was thirsty, but He was actually more concerned about her thirst than His.

When we trust in the gift of Jesus' grace, He gives us the living water, which is the Holy Spirit (Rom. 8:9), and if continue to rely on Him, we never need to thirst again. However, we are easily distracted. Therefore, we must continue to ask, and this reliance needs to become our ongoing disposition. This is very similar to what Jesus said to Peter when He said that even though he had "already bathed" (John 4:10), he would have to keep coming back to Jesus to have his feet washed. We must continue to live by the Spirit's power, and we do this by relying on the Spirit always.

Align Ourselves with God's Truth

When this woman returned to town to tell the people about the One she met, they came out to meet Jesus, and they prevailed on Jesus to stay with them a couple of days. And how precious those days must have been. There Jesus would convey truth to this woman, including the truth she would need to align her relationships according to God's truth. However, above all, she now knew the One who was the truth, and by the living water, His very Spirit, she would know Him always, and He would be for her a continual supply of His life.

Having said all of this, may I leave you with two simple applications from this chapter? The first is this: See Jesus as your greatest blessing. As you look to Him, see Him this way. Reflect on this often, and learn to rely on Him, more and more this way.

Then, as you see Him this way, let the living water of His Spirit flow into your spirit. If you will do these two things, then, as we will see in the next chapter, you will be ready to receive every blessing that flows out of the grace that comes from Him.

Summary

- Because Jesus is "the gift of God," He is also God's greatest gift and blessing to us.
- When we see "the gift of God" as we should, we see Jesus as we should. Because He came from the Father, He possesses the same nature as the Father, full of grace and truth.
- When we see "the gift of God" as we should, we also see the Father and the Sprit as we should. The Father, Son, and Holy Spirit are "triune" (three in one), which means they are distinguishable but inseparable. Because they are one, they also share in the same nature.

- When we see "the gift of God" as we should, we see grace as we should. Grace is the means to a higher end, which is to know Christ. It is also what the gift Jesus gives to us, like living water, so we will never thirst again.

- When we see the gift of God as we should, we see God's blessings as we should. God's blessings flow out of the grace of Christ. If we seek God's blessings above His grace, we will miss His grace and His blessings. If we seek grace above Christ, we will miss Christ, grace, and His blessings. However, if we seek Christ first, we will know Christ, His grace and His blessing.

- In order to know our greatest blessing, we must

  o Know the Gift of God
  o Ask for a Living Water
  o Align our Lives with God's truth.

Discussion Questions
for Chapter 4

1. Are there specific ways God spoke to you through this chapter?

2. Can you say you see the Father, Son, and Holy Spirit as all possessing the same nature? If not, how do you tend to see them differently? Why is it so important for us to see them as possessing the same nature?

3. Describe how it makes you to feel to know that God values you so much, He gave His Son to reconcile you to Himself.

4. Why does it matter that we see Jesus as an even greater blessing to us than the blessing of grace?

5. What did Jesus mean when He said the woman at the well would never thirst again if she drank the living water Jesus gave her?

6. What difference does it make in your life when you see Jesus as your very greatest blessing?

Assignment:

1. Memorize John 4:10

2. Make it your habit this week to Jesus as your very greatest blessing, and allow your heart to experience from Him the grace He pours out like living water by the Holy Spirit.

CHAPTER 5

The Grace of God in Every Blessing

In the last chapter, we learned something very important. As great as grace is, it is the means to a greater end, which is to know Christ. Then, when we know Him, He pours His grace into our lives. We can't seek grace apart from Christ because the very purpose of grace is to enable us to know Him. Then, when we know Him, we are able to experience the true grace that flows from Him. Then, only with this foundation in place are we able to know God's true blessings. There are multiple reasons for this.

Grace is the Beginning of Every Blessing

Before we can live in God's blessing, we must first receive His grace. Why?

To begin with, *the same heart we must possess to receive God's grace is the heart we must have to live in His blessing.* Grace is the soul of every blessing

God gives. This is something we see in the Priestly Blessing. At the very center of the blessing are the words God gave the priests to speak over the people: "and be gracious to you." This is what God wants to communicate about Himself. He is a gracious God. In this sense, in every blessing God gives, He is expressing His grace. Through His blessings, He is enabling us to experience His grace in an ongoing way, which is precisely what He wants for us. He wants His grace to be like the sun, lifted over us and shining on us always.

The question becomes, then: how are we going to live in the ongoing experience of God's grace if we have not received it to begin with? Again, the same heart we need to live in God's blessing is the heart we must have to receive His grace. We will never be able to live in God's blessing until we first receive His grace. This is why grace is the beginning of every blessing we receive from Him.

Here is a second reason: *God's unmerited favor is what moves us to merit His favor.* We have seen this relationship between unmerited and merited favor. God smiles on both, and both are expressed to us in the blessings God gives, but God's unmerited favor is what moves us to live in a way that merits His favor. Therefore, we must receive this unmerited favor, which is grace, first.

On this note, there is something that is interesting to me. We have seen how there are two separate words for merited and unmerited favor in the Old Testament, but there is just one word for both in the New Testament. It's the word *charis*. The context determines which one (merited or unmerited) it is referring to. And here is what is interesting to me about this. There is a sense in which we can't separate the two. Again, the unmerited favor is what produces the merited. But it's not that merited favor takes over where unmerited favor leaves off; unmerited favor never *leaves off.* here is never a time when merited favor doesn't depend on unmerited favor. This is true for two reasons. First, unmerited favor moves us to merit God's favor, but even when we begin to merit favor, we can never forget the unmerited favor we received at the start. And let's be honest. As long as we live in this life, we will always need God's unmerited favor because we continue to fall short, so we must continue to rely on unmerited favor always, and as we do, it continually moves us to merit God's favor. I believe this is how we should see this word charis in the New Testament. It is the fullness of grace that moves us to merit God's favor but never forgets merit favor, and it is the merited favor that never forgets the unmerited favor that produced it. Both merited and unmerited favor live together in *charis*, as they must live together in us.

And there is a third reason grace is the beginning of God's blessings in our lives: The grace we receive from God is what moves us to become instruments of His blessing in the lives of others. We have seen how moving it was for the disciples to allow Jesus to wash their feet, and what happened immediately after this is very significant as well. After returning to His place at the table, Jesus spoke these words to them:

> …. Do you know what I have done for you? You call Me Teacher and Lord, and rightly so, because I am. So if I, your Lord and Teacher, have washed your feet, you also should wash one another's feet. I have set you an example so that you should do as I have done for you. Truly, truly, I tell you, no servant is greater than his master, nor is a messenger greater than the one who sent him. If you know these things, you will be blessed if you do them. John 13:12-17

In this passage, we see an example of how important it is for us to receive *the grace of Christ*. When Jesus washed their feet, the thing that made it so impacting was the fact that He was their Teacher and Lord. The One who possessed perfect truth (their Teacher) served them in spite of all the ways they fell short of His truth. And the One who possessed all power and authority (their Lord) served them in their weakness.

The reason Jesus' disciples were to serve one another is because the One who was far greater served them. This is what also produced in them such a passion to do so. How could they fail to serve one another when their Teacher and Lord served them? And it was essential for them to let Him serve them this way because the only way they would ever learn to serve one another *as He served them* was by letting Him serve them.

I remember being so moved by this passage, I asked my older daughter one day: "What is your greatest responsibility before God?" She answered in a rather quizzical way, "To obey Him? I said, "No." She said, "To love Him?" I said, "No." "To serve Him?" "No." I said, "Your greatest responsibility before God is to let Him serve you."

> *"Your greatest responsibility before God is to let Him serve you"*

She said, "No…."

It's true though, and this is precisely what Jesus was teaching His disciples the night He washed their feet. Do we want to love God and live for Him? Do we want our service to have impact in the world? Do we want to know the blessing that comes from being a blessing? If so, one thing matters: we must allow the eternal God to serve us.

Then, as Jesus said, if His disciples would serve one another as He served them, they would be blessed. There was great blessing in the grace they received from Christ, but their blessing would only grow and multiply as they shared this same grace with one another.

Every blessing begins with grace. It's what gives us the heart to receive God's blessings; it's what moves us to live in a way that merits

His favor, and it's what moves us to serve others out of grace He has shown us.

Grace is the Essence of Every Blessing

Not only is grace the *beginning* of every blessing we receive from God, it is the *essence* of every blessing He gives, and there are some practical implications for us in this.

First, *we should guard against seeking God's blessings above the favor we experience in them.* This goes back to our definition for a blessing, which is: "a gift God gives as an expression of His favor." This makes God's favor the true essence of God's blessings. His blessing is not just in the gifts He gives, its in the favor He expresses in the gifts. So we must be careful to always experience His favor in the gifts, because the moment we lose the experience of His favor in the gifts He gives, their true blessing to us is lost.

On the occasion of our twenty-fifth wedding anniversary, my wife and I were more than blessed to celebrate on the beautiful Island of Maui. On one of our mornings there, we had breakfast at a restaurant near the ocean. I remember thinking about how each of my senses was engaged in some way. I heard the ocean water washing onto the shore in one wave after another (sound). There was the aroma of the ocean salt, which I have always loved (smell). On the table before me there was a variety of foods with the most amazing flavors (taste). I felt the warmth of the sun on my face and the sand on my feet (touch). And my eyes were dazzled by the most stunning beauty all around me (sight). Of course, the most beautiful sight was my wife across the table from me (yes, that is precisely what I was thinking…).

In that moment, I couldn't help but think: Why would God design the world the way He did if He didn't want us to experience His heart for us in all the gifts He has given us? And this is precisely what made all of these gifts such a blessing to me. It was the favor of God I experienced in them. If I lost the sense of His favor in these gifts though, their true blessing to me would be lost.

And there is something else we must remember as we attempt to keep God's grace tightly connected to the Person of Christ. God's very purpose for pouring His favor into us is to draw us to Himself. In Deut. 6:10-12, Moses spoke these words of warning to the Israelites just before they entered the Promised Land:

And when the LORD your God brings you into the land He swore to your fathers, to Abraham, Isaac, and Jacob, that He would give you—a land with great and splendid cities that you did not build, with houses full of every good thing with which you did not fill them, with wells that you did not dig, and with vineyards and olive groves that you did not plant—and when you eat and are satisfied, be careful not to forget the LORD who brought you out of the land of Egypt, out of the house of slavery.

Ironically, one of the greatest threats to our living in God's blessing is the blessings He gives us—if we love them more than we love Him. What then is the solution if we are tempted to value the gifts of God above the favor we experience in them? Is it to push away the gifts? Not at all. It is to be sure we experience God's favor in them and allow them to deepen our love for Him.

What then is the solution if we are tempted to value the gifts of God above the favor we experience in them? Is it to push away the gifts? Not at all. It is to be sure we experience God's favor in them and allow them to deepen our love for Him.

This is precisely what we see in the pages of Scripture. In Ps. 81:10 God says:

… Open wide your mouth,
    And I will fill it.

In Ps. 84:11, we read:

For the LORD God is a sun and a shield;
    the LORD gives grace and glory;

He withholds no good thing
    from those who walk with integrity.

In 1 Tim. 6:17, the apostle Paul says that God "richly provides all things for us to enjoy," and in 1 Tim. 4:3 He warns against listening to teachers who prohibit the good gifts "God has created to be received with thanksgiving by those who believe and know the truth." In Col. 2:23 he says that such teachings have the appearance of wisdom in self-made religion and self-abasement and severe treatment of the body; but they are of no value against the indulgence of the flesh.

With this goal in mind, there is one verse that can be of particular help to us. In Rom. 8:32, the apostle Paul writes:

For He who spared not His own Son, but gave Him up for us all, how will He not also, with Him, grant us all things? purpose for giving it.

This verse is incredibly rich and full of meaning. To begin with, the heart of God's love for us is revealed in the Son He gave for us, and if He loved us that much, how will He not, with Him, grant us all things? One of the most significant phrases in this verse though is "with Him." God does not give us His blessings apart from Christ, our greatest blessing. He gives them "with Him."

Understanding this can actually serve as a test for the blessings we seek. Do we see them as gifts God gives with Christ? If so, they will be received as gifts that enable us to sense His favor, and they will only increase out love for Him. And how beautiful it is for us to pursue the gifts God give "with Him." In Pr. 24:3-4 we read:

> By wisdom a house is built
> > and by understanding it is established;
>
> through knowledge its rooms are filled
> > with every precious and beautiful treasure.

There is another practical implication for us in realizing that the grace of Christ is the essence of every blessing. *We can experience God's blessings apart any material gift at all.*

When I was beginning to gather together the thoughts that would go into this discipleship curriculum, some friends invited us to spend a couple of weeks at a vacation home they own in Colorado. (You may be getting the impression that Jeanie and I travel all the time. I would mind that, but it's not actually true….) One of our days there, we went for a hike on a high mountain trail, and I began to have many of the same feelings had on our trip to Hawaii. As I observed the most incredible beauty all around me, as I listened to the birds in the trees, as I drew in the scent of the mountain pines, as I breathed in the crisp, cool air, I felt as if God's very heart was pounding with the desire to bless us with the creation He placed us in.

When we returned to our friends' home, I tried to make some progress on this book, but unfortunately, I experienced a very severe "writer's block." As hard as I tried, and as eager as I was to convey the things I was feeling, the words were not coming. This is when I decided to pause and simply experience the things I was trying to convey. I moved over to a large chair in front of a window that looked out on a large mountain. Then, after a few moments of simply being still, I asked God to allow me to experience in a fresh way, the fullness of His grace.

It had to be intentional about this, because this doesn't come naturally for me. Instead of trying to produce anything, I simply attempted to receive. With this new posture in my heart, I began to confess to God anything I could think of that fell short of His glory in my life. As I did this, I simply relied on His grace, and even when I couldn't think of anything else to confess, I asked Him to cleanse me of things I was not even aware of. Then, somehow I felt as if His grace was washing over with one wave after another.

It's hard to convey what this was like. All I can say is that, after two hours, I didn't want it to stop. I felt as if I could stay right there forever. I had this distinct feeling that I didn't need anything else in this world except grace. If I have a roof over my head and food on the table, His grace would be enough.

This experience was so powerful, I wondered if I had ever known true grace before. I realized though that this is something we all must keep growing in. And I was simply grateful for the grace God allowed me to grow in that day.

Since this time, I have come to see writer's block in a different way. It is still frustrating, but I am growing to see it as God's call to experience what I am trying to convey.

Not long after this, I was back at home in the room we set aside for an office, and I found myself in a similar place. The words wouldn't come. Again, I decided to use the same strategy. I would simply wait on God.

This is also incredibly hard for me to convey, but this time what I experienced was even more powerful. I felt it was the very Person of Christ, present there and pouring His grace into me. Just like before, I didn't want to move. After another two hours, I didn't it this to end.

All I can say is that, as great as grace is, the Christ from whom it comes is greater.

Based on these experiences, I have come to believe there is a simple way to describe what it means "to live in the blessing": it is simply to live in grace. And there is another, even simpler way to say it: to live in the blessing is to live in Christ.

> *to live in the blessing is to live in Christ.*

To know Christ as our greatest blessing is beautiful, because He can never be taken from us, and He gives us the promise that in seeking first God's kingdom and His righteousness, we will always possess all that we truly need (Matt. 6:33).

There is still another implication for us that comes from understanding that grace is the true essence of every blessing.

We can experience God's blessings even in the midst of our greatest trials. In 2 Cor. 12:5-10, the apostle Paul speaks of a "thorn" in his flesh. We are not told what it was, but it was so painful he prayed three times for God to remove it. God chose not to remove it though. Because Paul had experienced so many visions from God, he could have easily become conceited. Therefore, God gave him the thorn to keep him humble. And in 2 Cor. 12:9 we see His reply:

> But He said to me, "My grace is sufficient for you, for My power is perfected in weakness" ....

Even in the midst of our sufferings, the grace we experience from Him is so powerful, it actually perfects His power in us. When Paul experienced this new power, he said:

> ... Therefore I will boast all the more gladly in my weaknesses, so that the power of Christ may rest on me. That is why, for

the sake of Christ, I delight in weaknesses, in insults, in hardships, in persecutions, in difficulties. For when I am weak, then I am strong. 2 Cor. 12:9-10

When suffering is endured out of faithfulness to Christ, the favor we experience outweighs the pain of our trials. Because of the grace Paul experienced in the trials he endured, if he had to choose between *suffering with grace* and *no suffering with no grace*, he would have chosen the suffering with the grace, because the grace was so powerful to him—and produced such great power in him.

There is something else we should not overlook in this passage. In Paul's time of need, it was not just grace that was sufficient; it was the grace that issued forth from the Person of Christ. Jesus said, "My grace is sufficient for you." What He experienced was more than grace; he experienced the life of Christ in the grace poured into Him. And this was *greater* than all His sufferings.

Not only is the grace of Christ the beginning of every blessing and the essence of every blessing we receive, there is one more thing we need to emphasize.

Grace is the Greatest Blessing of Eternal Life

What is the greatest blessing we will know in heaven? The Bible speaks of many beautiful things about that place, including streets of gold (Rev. 21:21), a great banquet (Matt. 8:11), dwelling places Jesus Himself is preparing for us (John 14:1-3). In heaven there will be no tears, death, mourning, or pain (Rev. 21:4).

The glory of heaven is something we can only imagine, but as great as it will be, I am convinced that the greatest blessing we *experience* there is the eternal, unbroken and undiminished grace of God poured into our hearts—forever.

In 1 Pet. 1:13 Peter said:

> … Set your hope fully on the grace to be given you at the revelation of Jesus Christ.

Why should we set our hope fully on the grace to given us? His grace is the only means by which we will enter, but there is another reason. His grace will be our greatest experience of blessing there.

Above all, this is what Peter longed for, and there is something I find very moving about the life of Peter. According to early church history, he lived the latter part of his life in Rome. There, he carried out Jesus' call to feed His sheep (John 21:15-17), and there he was eventually martyred.[9]

What then can we draw from this chapter? What I have in mind is the reverse of what I shared with you in the last chapter. The application in the last chapter was, first, to see Jesus as our very greatest blessing. Then, it was to let His grace pour into our hearts like living water.

Here is the objective for this chapter: First, be sure to experience His grace in every gift He gives. The true essence of the blessing is favor, so let this favor, which always begins with grace, pour into you, and seek from Him gifts that enable you to experience His favor.

Then, let this favor accomplish its purpose, which is to join you to the living Christ. The ultimate goal, higher than everything, is to know Him, and when we do, His favor will continually be poured into us.

There, the only song greater than our song of praise to Him will be the song of His pleasure over us.

In heaven, Jesus will be the light by which we see, and in His light, we will experience the fullness of His grace, like the

---

[9] The apostle John alludes to this in John 21:19.

light of His countenance lifted up over us. There, the only song greater than our song of praise to Him will be the song of His pleasure over us—and only because His songs are always greater than ours.

In Luke 12:37 we read something that genuinely humbles me. There Jesus says:

> Blessed are those servants whom the master finds on watch when he returns. Truly I tell you, he will dress himself to serve and will have them recline at the table, and he himself will come and wait on them. Luke 12:37

This is something I overlooked for a long time. Even in heaven, Jesus will wait on us. How can this be? Hasn't He served us enough? His nature never changes though, and even there He will continue to serve us. As Jesus said, how blessed those servants will be. He will serve them, and we can be sure they will serve Him in return. There we will live in the mutual relationship of blessing He created us for.

There is something else we should remember about eternal life. As we saw in the last chapter, this is the life we possess in Christ even now, because Christ Himself is eternal life. How beautiful this is for us to realize. We have this eternal life living in us now, and no, it is not complete in us because our flesh interferes with its fullness. It is a deposit of the fullness that is to come. Therefore, how powerful it is to allow this grace of Christ to fill us now. We do this when we remember the grace we have received, when we live in its fullness today, and when we realize we will live in its totality one day.

So what can we take from this chapter and apply to our lives? What I have in mind is the reverse of what I shared with you in the last chapter. The application in the last chapter was, first, to see Jesus as our very greatest blessing. Then, it was to let His grace pour into our hearts like living water that comes from Him.

Here is the goal today. Be sure to experience His grace in everything. The true essence of the blessing is favor, so let this favor, which always begins with grace, pour into you through every blessing He gives. Experience the favor of God in all the gifts He has given, and seek from Him gifts that enable you to experience His favor. Let this favor pour into you.

Then, secondly, let this favor accomplish its purpose, which is to join you to the living Christ. The ultimate goal, higher than everything, is to know Him, and when we do, His favor will continually be poured into us.

With these two things in mind, let me communicate this one last thing. In 2 Pet. 1:13-15, the apostle Peter writes:

> I think it is right to refresh your memory as long as I live in the tent of my body, because I know that this tent will soon be laid aside, as our Lord Jesus Christ has made clear to me. And I will make every effort to ensure that after my departure, you will be able to recall these things at all times.

Here we see the reason Peter wrote this letter. He realized he would soon step across to the other side, as the Lord Jesus Christ had somehow made clear to him. He wants to leave us all with a reminder of the most important things, so what would he write?

In the very last verse of this letter, we read the last words we have from Peter in our New Testament. They come from the one who used to boast in himself, until his life was forever changed by the grace of Christ. He writes:

> But grow in the grace and knowledge of our Lord and Savior Jesus Christ. To Him be the glory, both now and to the age of eternity. Amen. 2 Pet. 3:18

Summary

- The grace of Christ is the beginning of every blessing because:

    o We can never know God's heart of grace in the blessings He gives unless we are first able to receive His heart of grace.

    o God's unmerited favor (grace) is what moves us to live in a way that merits His favor.

    o Grace moves us to become instruments of His blessing in the lives of others.

- The grace of Christ is the essence of every blessing God gives, and there are important implications for this:

    o We should guard against seeking God's blessings above the grace of Christ.

    o We can experience God's blessings apart any material gift at all.

    o We can experience God's blessings even in the midst of our greatest trials.

- The Grace of Christ is the Greatest Blessing of Eternal Life
- There is no greater objective we can devote ourselves to than to grow in the grace and knowledge of our Lord Jesus Christ.

Discussion Questions
for Chapter 5

1. Were there ways God spoke to you through this lesson?

2. Why is it so easy to for us to love the blessings God gives above the God who gives them? How can we guard against allowing this to happen?

3. Can you think of a time when you experienced true blessing from God apart from any material thing?

4. Can you think of a time when a trial you went through increased your experience of grace and your knowledge of Christ?

5. What do you look forward to most in heaven?

6. How can you begin even now, to experience the eternal
    life that is in Jesus alone?

Assignment:

1. Memorize 2 Pet. 3:18

2. This week, allow your heart to experience the grace of
    God through the blessings He has given you, whether ma-
    terial or otherwise. Then, let the grace you experience
    draw you to give thanks to the One who gave it.

CHAPTER 6

The Fullness of God's Blessing

I heard about a preacher who loved to play golf, but he wanted the members of His church to be present on Sundays, so he preached often that they should save their golf game for another day. And even when they were on vacation he wanted them to be in church somewhere—and he made this known as well. Then, one weekend, when he was out of town, he had a chance to play a round of golf, but his only opportunity was on Sunday morning, and so, contrary to everything he had preached, he decided to play golf that day, but he did it alone....

At this time the angel Gabriel was standing next the Lord and said, "Lord, what should we do about this?"

The Lord said, "I've got it...."

When the preacher teed off on the very first hole, a long par four, God sent a rush of wind that carried the ball all the way to the green. It landed a few yards from the cup and rolled directly in—a double eagle. Gabriel said, "Lord, why did you do that? Shouldn't you punish him?" And the Lord said, "I did punish him. Who's he going to be able to tell?"

It can be almost painful not to be able to tell someone about something really great that happens to us. And this applies to virtually anything. It could be a movie we see, a book we read, a new restaurant we discover.... We have to tell somebody.

This is why Jesus' apostles turned their world upside down. Most simply put, they experienced something so great they couldn't keep it to themselves. The apostle John writes about this in 1 John 1:3-4:

> We proclaim to you what we have seen and heard, so that you also may have fellowship with us. And this fellowship of ours is with the Father and with His Son, Jesus Christ. We write these things so that our joy may be complete.

John was moved to write this letter so his own joy would be complete, and this is true of all of God's blessings. Our joy only increases when we share them with others.

Interestingly, in both the Old and New Testaments, there are distinct words for *expressing* a blessing and *experiencing* a blessing, and it's helpful to understand the meaning of each one.

The Expression and Experience of Blessing

In Chapter One we learned the Hebrew for a blessing God *expresses* to us. It's the word *barak*, which means "to kneel." This is the same word used for a blessing we *express* to Him as well.

The Hebrew word for the *experience* of a blessing is *esher* (eh'-sher). To give an example, In Ps. 119:1 we read:

> Blessed [*esher*] are those whose way is blameless,
>   who walk in the Law of the LORD.

This word comes from the Hebrew word *ashar* (aw-shar'), which means "to continue on a straight path," so what does this have to do with *experiencing* God's blessing? One of the best ways to explain this is to return to the prayer the Jewish people prayed when they blessed God for their bread:

> Blessed are You, Lord God, King of the universe, who brings forth bread from the earth.

As we have seen, the people recognized that only the King of the universe could design the earth with the capacity to bring forth bread, but they also realized what was required of them. They had to align their lives with way God designed the earth (by working the land) if they were going to draw forth its blessings. Their alignment with God's created order was the "straight path" they had to continue in.

This is why the Bible speaks so consistently of the blessing that comes from keeping God's laws. To begin with, there are natural laws that govern His universe, and only when we align our lives with those laws are we able to derive its benefits. If we understood this as we should, we would never see God's laws as harsh or oppressive; we would see them as our opportunities to draw forth His blessings from the earth. And just as there are natural laws that govern the universe, there are also spiritual and relational "laws" that we must respect.

In John 10:35 Jesus said, "… the Scripture cannot be broken." This really surprised me when I first read it. I thought: "It seems like people break the Scripture all the time." In a sense this is true, but not in the sense Jesus was talking about. Suppose a man jumps from a high building and yells out: "Look everyone, I'm breaking the law of gravity!" Not re-

if we try to break God's laws, His laws eventually break us.

ally…. The law of gravity is about to break Him. In this sense we can't break God's laws; if we try to break God's laws, His laws eventually break us. Only when we align our lives with God's truth will we *experience* the blessing God wishes to *express* to us.

In the New Testament, the Greek word for the *expression* of blessing is *eulogeo* (yoo-log-eh'-o), which literally means "good (*eu*) word (*logeo*)." This shouldn't surprise us, given the fact that many blessings in the Old Testament consist of spoken words. It is also used though for any expression of blessing, whether spoken or not.

This is the word used for the time when Jesus took little children in His arms, placed His hands on them, and "blessed" them (Mark 10:16). This could mean He spoke a word of blessing over them, but it could also mean the children received a blessing from simply being held by Him. There is a sense in which all of God's blessings speak to us in some way, even if the blessing is unspoken, because every blessing He gives expresses His favor to us.[10]

The word for the *experience* of God's blessing in the New Testament is *makarios* (mak-ar'-ee-os).[11] This is the word Jesus used in the *Beatitudes*. For example, in Matt. 5:9 He says:

Blessed are the peacemakers, for they will be called sons of God. (Matt. 5:9)

This word is drawn from the Greek word *mak*, which means, "extended, long, large." We get our prefix "macro" from this word. It

---

[10] This is also the word used in Mark 6:41 for the "blessing" Jesus spoke before feeding the 5000. We have every reason to believe He expressed the same prayer the Jewish people continue to pray to bless God for their food in our day—or similar to it. Some translations say He blessed the food, but this is not in the original language, and the verse states that He looked to heaven as He spoke the blessing.

[11] It's significant to note that when the New Testament authors translated an Old Testament verse from Hebrew to Greek, they used the word *eulogia* to translate *barak* (Matt. 23:39 and Ps. 118:26) and they used *macarios* to translate *esher* (Rom. 4:7-8 and Ps. 32:1-2).

speaks of the extension of God's grace toward us. Every blessing we experience is an extension of His grace to us, and it is also the way He enables us to experience His grace in an ongoing way.

> Every blessing we experience is an extension of His grace to us

Some versions of the Bible translate this word "happy," but this does not take into account the emphasis in Scripture on favor in God's blessings. Happiness depends on the "happenings" in our lives, but our experience of God's favor within us doesn't depend on the circumstances (happenings) around us.

By way of summary, here are the primary biblical terms for blessing in the Old and New Testaments:

	Old Testament (Hebrew)	New Testament (Greek)
Expression	Barak (to kneel)	Eulogia (good word)
Experience	Esher (continue in a straight path)	Makarios (long, extended)

As we learned in the first chapter, one of the characteristics of God's blessings is that they are more than we can contain. When we have *received* God's blessing, we must *respond* in some way. Another way we can say this is that we must *express* what we have *experienced*. God's blessing begins with what He expresses to us. He is the One who bows low to bless us with the gifts He gives. This is what moves us to respond by blessing Him in return, both upwardly and outwardly, and these two responses produce the "full volume" of God's blessing in our lives. Perhaps some visuals will help convey this.

The Full Volume of God's Blessing

First, when we experience a blessing God expresses to us, our experience of His blessing moves us to respond by expressing our praise and thanksgiving to Him.

This upward response on our part is vital, and this is a good place to summarize the reasons it is so essential.

Our Upward Response:

Gives Evidence that we have been Blessed. In Luke 17:11-19 we learn about Jesus' encounter with ten lepers. When they saw Him, they cried out for Him to have mercy on them. Jesus told them to show themselves to the priests, which required under the law for those who had been healed of a skin disease (Lev. 14:1-32). On their way to the priests, they were all cleansed of their leprosy, but only one, a Samaritan, returned to thank Jesus. On that day, ten received the gift of God, but only one received the blessing. Why? The blessing is not in the gift alone; it is in the favor we experience in the gift, and when we experience this favor, we are moved to respond by expressing our praise and thanks to God. This is the evidence we have truly received the blessing.

Is how we Give to God and Bless Him. When this one leper returned to give thanks, Jesus asked, "Where are the other nine?" As I read these words, I can't help but wonder how often God's heart is broken by our ingratitude. We all know the sting of ingratitude, but we can't begin to know how often God has felt this pain. On the other hand, our praise and gratitude bring great pleasure to Him. As we have seen, there is one thing God will never possess unless we give it to Him: our hearts. And when we give God our hearts, it brings great blessing to Him.

Makes our Blessing Complete. As great as the Samaritan's gratitude was, it would not be complete until He expressed His gratitude to Jesus. Until He did this, He would feel a debt of gratitude in his soul. With the payment of this "debt" though, his joy would be made full. God's very purpose for blessing him would also be fulfilled, which was to draw this man to Himself.

How beautiful this union is between our lives and the life of God. This is what God created us for, and this is also what moves us to express to others, outwardly, what He has done for us. We can see this as a horizontal plain that moves out from us in every direction:

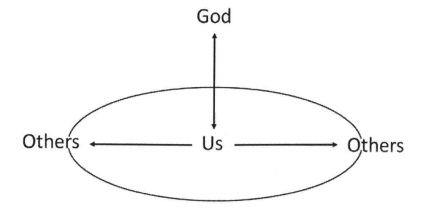

Even when we know the joy of blessing God upwardly, our blessing will not be complete apart from the blessing we express to others outwardly. This is why the apostle John said, "We write these things so that our joy may be complete (1 John 1:4). And very significantly, the very same things that apply to our upward response apply also to our outward response.

Our Outward Response:

Gives Evidence that we have been Blessed

In the book of Isaiah, God expresses His great displeasure over the meaningless sacrifices the people were bringing Him. He found "no delight" in them (Is. 1:11), and He was actually "weary" of them (Is. 1:14). Why? Their upward devotion to Him was producing no outward service to others. In Is. 1:16-17 He says:

Wash and cleanse yourselves.
> Remove your evil deeds from My sight.
> Stop doing evil!

Learn to do right;
> seek justice and correct the oppressor.

Defend the fatherless
> and plead the case of the widow."

This reminds us of the words of the apostle James in in Jas. 1:27:

Pure and undefiled religion before our God and Father is this: to care for orphans and widows in their distress, and to keep oneself from being polluted by the world.

What did this mean? It meant that whatever outward forms our upward expression of worship to God may take, it is not pleasing to

God and it is not even real if it does not result in outward expression to others.

If we have been touched by the blessing of God, it will result, not just in praise and thanksgiving to God, but also in outward service to

If we have been touched by the blessing of God, it will result, not just in praise and thanksgiving to God, but also in outward service to others.

others. The result will never be one or the other; it's always both.

Is how we Give to God and Bless Him. In Matt. 25:34-40, Jesus gives us the following picture of what will take place when we stand before Him in judgment one day:

Then the King [Jesus] will say to those on His right, 'Come, you who are blessed by My Father, inherit the kingdom prepared for you from the foundation of the world. For I was hungry and you gave Me something to eat, I was thirsty and you gave Me something to drink, I was a stranger and you took Me in, I was naked and you clothed Me, I was sick and you looked after Me, I was in prison and you visited Me.'

Then the righteous will answer Him, 'Lord, when did we see You hungry and feed You, or thirsty and give You something to drink? When did we see You a stranger and take You in, or naked and clothe You? When did we see You sick or in prison and visit You?'

And the King will reply, 'Truly I tell you, whatever you did for one of the least of these brothers of Mine, you did for Me.'

This shows us how God sees the gifts we give to others. They are gifts to Him as well, and this also brings blessing to Him. Just before this parable, Jesus gives another parable about two stewards who were faithful to what their master entrusted to them, and one who was not.

The master had the strongest words of retribution for the servant who did nothing with what he was entrusted with (Matt. 25:26-29), but He had the highest words of commendation for the two faithful servants.

> Well done, good and faithful servant! You have been faithful with a few things; I will put you in charge of many things. Enter into the joy of your master! (Matt. 25:21, 23).

Based on the relationship between these two parables, we can see what God seeks in our faithful stewardship. It's what we do to serve others.

Makes our Blessing Complete. The pleasure we give to God is what makes our pleasure truly complete, and the blessing we give to God is what makes our blessing complete.

One of the things the apostle Paul was moved to do during his third missionary journey was to collect an offering for the poor in Jerusalem. The believers in Corinth participated in this, and Paul affirmed them for it, as we see in 2 Cor. 9:12:

> For this ministry of service is not only supplying the needs of the saints, but is also overflowing in many expressions of thanksgiving to God.

Can you imagine how gratifying it was for the believers in Corinth to realize there were people they had never known who would bow their knees before the Father and give thanks to Him for gifts they had sent them? What could be more rewarding than this?

Jesus said, "It is more blessed to give than to receive (Acts 20:35)," and why is this? Our sense of blessing comes from the favor we experience from God, and the favor we experience from Him only grows as we share with others the blessings we have received from Him.

One day, when our daughter Brittany was in kindergarten, she brought home a picture she colored at school. It had our house and green grass to each side of it. The sun was in the top left corner. Standing outside the house were all the members of our family, including our dog—that would be Buster. She was very proud to show it to us, and even though it would not have won any art prizes, it won a prize in our hearts. We put it on our refrigerator and made a big deal of it. We told her how great it was, and we could see she had no greater pleasure than knowing we were pleased with it.

And there is no greater pleasure we can have than knowing we have brought pleasure to the heart of God. To receive God's blessing is *good*, and to bless others is *better*, but to bless God is the *best* and greatest blessing we can know.

> *To receive God's blessing is good, and to bless others is better, but to bless God is the best and greatest blessing we can know.*

One day, nothing will mean more to us than knowing our lives have brought pleasure to our Lord. If we truly understood this, we would live all of our days for the sake of that day. And the important thing for us to remember is that it is our service to others that brings pleasure to Him.

One day, when we stand before Him, He will not say, "Well received, good and faithful recipient." His only words of commendation will be, "Well done, good and faithful servant."

> *One day, when we stand before Him, He will not say, "Well received, good and faithful recipient."*

This is what produces the full volume of God's blessing in our lives. Even in the material realm, the combination of the one dimension of a vertical line (height) with the two dimensions of a horizontal plane (length and width) produces the three dimensions of volume.

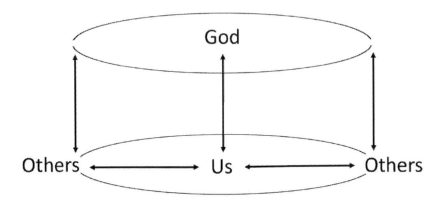

As we think about the "volume" that is produced when the blessing of God comes to us and then moves us to respond both upwardly and outwardly, we might picture a downward stream of water filling the center of a pool. The initial impact results in an upward splash. However, the ongoing stream pushes the water outward in all directions. Then, the entire water level begins to rise.

In this analogy, we can see God being blessed at every point. He is blessed when we receive the blessing He gives, and He is blessed when we praise and thank Him in return. Then, He is blessed to see us give to others, and He is blessed by what others receive from us. He is blessed again when others are moved to bless Him for the blessings they have received from Him through us. All of this brings great blessing to God, and this is what makes *our* sense of blessing so full.

There is more though....

We have to remember that those who bless God for the blessing they receive from us are moved to bless others as well, and now the pool only expands:

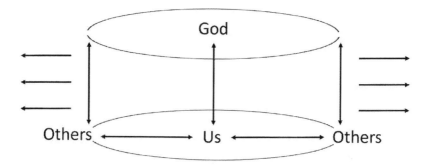

The beautiful thing about this is that the expansion of this "pool" is virtually limitless. As it expands, perhaps we should begin to see it as a lake, and then it only continues to grow until we have to see ourselves swimming in a veritable ocean of God's blessing.

This is what happens when we share with others the blessing we have received from God, and because Jesus is the greatest blessing we could ever receive from the Father, there is no greater blessing we could ever share than Him.[12]

You may be thinking by now: that sounds wonderful. I would love to live in the blessing of God that is that full. Is this really possible though? How could God ever work in me or use me to the extent that this blessing could expand or reach out to bless the world?

If this is where you are, let me remind you of this one thing. We can do nothing until we receive, but when we truly receive, God will move us to do the rest. Therefore, our focus doesn't have to be on

---

[12] This is the focus of Book Two, Chapter Seven: Sharing our Greatest Blessing.

how widely the blessing goes out; it simply needs to be on how deeply we receive it.

This doesn't mean we don't need to take the initiative to give thanks and praise to God or to serve others. When we do these things, our own sense of blessing is rekindled. The fullness of our expressing, though, is birthed in the fullness of our experiencing.

If we will fully receive God's blessing, then we will share it.

We just can't help it....

Summary

- There are distinct words for the *expression* and *experience* of a blessing in the Old and New Testaments. Although it is not important for us to remember the actual words from the original language, it is important to understand that what God expresses to us does not become complete until we, by faith, allow it to become our experience. Only then will we be moved to express to God and to others our response for the what we experienced.
- The fullness of blessing begins with receiving. If we will truly receive, then we will respond in praise to God, and we will also respond outwardly to others. Both responses:
- Are evidence we have received His blessing
- Are ways we give to God and bring blessing to Him
- Make our blessing complete.
- To receive God's blessing is good, to bless others is better, and to bless God is the best and greatest blessing we can experience.
- When we share God's blessings with others, there is no limit to it's expansion, which only blesses us more.

- We would do well to fix our sights on the day we will stand before the Lord, and we should live our days here for the sake of that day.
- Nothing will mean more to us when we stand before the Lord than knowing we have brought blessing to Him.

Discussion Questions
for Chapter 6

1. Are there ways God spoke to you through this Chapter?

2. What are the four words that are used for blessing in the Bible. Describe the significance of each.

3. Why did Jesus say that we are unable to break Scripture?

4. Give an example of how we are able to draw forth God's blessings from God's created order when we respect the truth He has created in it?

5. Have you ever experienced a distinct change in your life because of a word of blessing someone spoke to you? Describe this.

6. What is the greatest thing we can hear from God when we stand before Him one day?

7. Knowing this, what are some specific ways this affects our daily lives?

Assignment:

1. Memorize James 1:27.

2. Ask God to place on your heart a person you can serve as an expression of a blessing from Him. You may want to do this without letting this person know who is serving them, if possible, or you may want to let this person know if it will help this person experience God's favor in the blessing you give.

CHAPTER 7

The Faith God Blesses

Of all the people we read about in the Bible, who was the most blessed? I'm speaking now of mere mortals—everyone other than the Lord Jesus Himself.

Was it Abraham?

God called Abraham to leave his country, his relatives, and his father's household, and to go to the land He would show him (Gen. 12:1). And this call was accompanied by a promise. God said:

I will make you into a great nation,
  and I will bless you;

I will make your name great,
  so that you will be a blessing.

I will bless those who bless you
  and curse those who curse you;

and all the families of the earth
  will be blessed through you. (Gen. 12:2-3)

In the next verse we see why Abraham (whose name was originally Abram) actually realized the great blessing God promised him: "So Abram went forth as the LORD had spoken to him.... (Gen. 12:4 NASB)." As Jesus said, God blesses those who hear and obey His word (Luke 11:28), and this is precisely what Abraham did.

Or was it Moses?

God called Moses to deliver the Israelites from their bondage in Egypt (Ex. 3:10), and God gave the people His laws through Moses (Ex. 24:12). God spoke to Moses "face to face," just as a man speaks to his friend (Ex. 33:11). After being in God's presence, Moses' face would shine with the light he saw in God's face (Ex. 34:35). As we have seen, God's blessing is in His favor, and we experience God's favor in the light of His countenance. Who then received the experience of God's favor more than Moses did?

Or should we say it was David?

David became the King of Israel because God was seeking "a man after His own heart" (1 Sam. 13:14). He was careful to hear and obey God's word (2 Sam. 5:22-25). This is why God blessed Him (Ps. 65:4), and this is why so many of the Psalms David wrote express the blessing he gave to God (e.g. Ps. 16:7). So blessed was David that God promised he would never lack a descendant to sit on his throne (2 Sam. 7:8-17, 1 Kings 8:25-26), and this promise was supremely fulfilled in Jesus (Luke 1:32).

Or was it Peter?

Jesus had twelve disciples, and Peter was one of the three who was a part of His inner circle (e.g. Mark 5:37, Matt. 17:1). Peter Himself was the leader among the three. His name was originally Simon, but Jesus changed it to Peter (John 1:42), which means "rock." This was because of the unique role he would have in extending God's kingdom, which would be like a rock that nothing could withstand (Dan. 2:44-45, Matt. 16:18).

When Jesus asked His disciples to identify who He was, Peter said, "You are the Christ, the Son of the living God (Matt. 16:16)." In response, Jesus said:

> Blessed are you, Simon son of Jonah! For this was not revealed to you by flesh and blood, but by My Father in heaven. (Matt. 16:17)

Was Paul the most blessed?

Paul persecuted the church early in his life, but after God saved him, he never forgot the grace God showed him. Because of the grace he received, he actually worked harder than the other apostles (1 Cor. 15:10). He also authored more books in our New Testament than anyone,13 In Eph. 1:3, Paul writes:

> Blessed be the God and Father of our Lord Jesus Christ, who has blessed us in Christ with every spiritual blessing in the heavenly realms.

Paul's letters bear witness that he experienced this rich blessing of God in his life.

These are just a few examples of individuals who were greatly blessed by God, and we could add many more. Of all the saints throughout all of time, who was the most blessed?

I have a picture in my mind of a great crowd standing before the Lord, and He is about to ask the most blessed to step forward. To begin with, he motions for Abraham to step aside. Then He says the

---

[13] The author of the Book of Hebrews is unnamed, but if Paul wrote this book, then he wrote a total of fourteen.

same to Moses and David. Then he tells Peter and Paul to step aside as well.

Then, finally, He motions for a young woman in the middle of the crowd. She is perhaps no more than fourteen years of age, and He says, "Mary, step forward."

Again, this is a picture in my own mind, but why do I see it this way? It's because of all the people who have ever lived, Mary was utterly unique. In her was conceived the life of the very Son of God, and through her, God's greatest gift and blessing to us would enter the world.

This brings up a question though. Is it even appropriate to ask who among all mortals is most blessed?

This question is worth asking because it points to a deeper question. As we have seen, the essence of every blessing is the *favor* we experience in the gifts God gives. Therefore, we must ask: "Does God favor one person over another?"

Our initial response might be to say that God would never favor one person over another because He shows no favoritism (Rom. 2:11, Acts 10:34, Gal. 2:6). However, to show favoritism is show favor on an *inappropriate* basis. For example, to favor someone on the basis of wealth or status because of their ability to benefit us in some way is never appropriate (Jas. 2:1-4). However, it's an entirely different thing to show favor on an *appropriate* basis.

One of the things we have seen multiple times now is that favor can be both unmerited and merited. And throughout Scripture, we see one thing that merits God's favor more than anything: faith. This is what Jesus looked for more than anything in the lives of those He healed (e.g. Matt. 9:22, Mark 10:52, Luke 17:19). In Matt. 9:29, He said, "According to your faith will it be done to you." This speaks of a "measure" of faith. In Rom. 12:3, the apostle Paul said that we should regard ourselves according to the measure of faith God has given us. And in Matt. 8:19, Jesus praises the faith of a Gentile centurion who possessed greater faith than anyone in Israel.

If God favors faith, and if there are differing levels of faith, doesn't it stand to reason that some are more highly favored by Him than others? God does not show favoritism, but He favors those who have faith, and this is the only way I can explain the favor He showed Mary. It must have been because of her great faith.

> *God does not show favoritism, but He favors those who have faith*

Interestingly, in the first chapter of Luke, there is a very clear contrast between Mary and a relative of hers named Zechariah. Zechariah was a priest, and as he was carrying out his work in the temple one day, the angel Gabriel revealed to him that he would be the father of the forerunner of the Christ, whom we know as John the Baptist (Luke 1:11-17). When Zechariah heard this, he asked the angel how he could be sure this would happen (Luke 1:18). This question was displeasing to God though because it demonstrated a lack of faith. Therefore, as a consequence, he would unable to speak until the day his son was born (Luke 1:20).

Later, when Gabriel revealed to Mary that she would give birth to the very Son of God, she also had a question. She asked how this could happen, given the fact that she was a virgin (Luke 1:34). However, her question was not rooted in a lack of faith. She was simply seeking understanding. The angel explained that the Holy Spirit would come upon her, and the power of the Most High would overshadow her, so the Holy One born to her would be called the Son of God (Luke 1:35). The angel continued, "For no word from God will ever fail (Luke 1:37)." Then we see Mary's humble response of faith:

"I am the Lord's servant.... May it happen to me according to
your word." (Luke 1:38)

Soon after this, Mary went to visit Elizabeth, the wife of Zechariah,
and we see very clearly how pleasing Mary's faith was to God in the
words Elizabeth spoke to her:

Blessed is she who has believed that the Lord's word to her will
be fulfilled. (Luke 1:45)

Why did Mary find favor in God's sight? It was because of her faith.
She believed that the Lord's word to her would be fulfilled, and in her
we see beautiful characteristics of the faith God chooses to bless.

The Faith God Blesses:

Trusts in His Nature

In Heb. 11:6 we read:

And without faith it is impossible to please God, because anyone who approaches Him must believe that He exists and that
He rewards those who earnestly seek Him.

Faith consists of more than believing God exists; it includes believing something about His nature. He "rewards" those who earnestly
seek Him, and there are two things we must believe about God if we
believe He will reward us. First, we must believe He is *strong* enough to
reward us, and second, we must believe He is *good* enough.

When I was very young, as I played in the backyard of my home,
my Frisbee and Hula Hoop would often find their way to the roof of
our house. When this happened, Dad would lift me up high enough to
climb on the roof so I could retrieve my prized toys. I found the roof
to be an incredibly fun place to be (which explains why my Frisbee and
Hula Hoop ended up on the roof so often...). There was one thing I

loved more than anything though about my rooftop experiences. After throwing my toys down to the yard below, I would stand at the edge of the roof, with my Dad standing directly below me, and when I was sure he was ready, I would leap into his arms with the utmost abandon.

Of course, I wasn't thinking about this at the time, but there were two things that enabled me to jump. First, I had to believe Dad was *strong* enough to catch me. If Mom had been down there, I wouldn't have jumped.... Second, I had to believe he was *good* enough. If my brother had been down there, I sure wouldn't have jumped....

In a similar way, the reason we obey is because we believe God is good enough and strong enough to do what is best for us. This is the essence of genuine faith, and it is the root of all of our obedience. When we obey God it's because we have faith, and when we disobey, it's because we lack faith. To say this another way, when we fail to obey, it's because we don't trust in God's power or goodness—or both. This is

> *our faith brings great pleasure to God because it honors Him as the God of all power and goodness.*

also the reason our lack of faith is so displeasing to God. Our lack of faith is actually an insult to Him because it questions His very nature. However, our faith brings great pleasure to God because it honors Him as the God of all power and goodness.[14]

---

[14] Interestingly, we can see God's goodness as the combination of His love (*checed*) and truth (*emeth*). For example, in Ps. 100:5 we read: "For the LORD is good; His lovingkindness [*checed*] is everlasting And His faithfulness [*emeth*] to all generations (NASB)." (*Emeth* is sometimes translated "faithfulness" because God is faithful to His truth.) Drawing from God's three primary attributes: power, truth, and love, and then combining truth and love into goodness, we can say that our trust in God's strength and goodness is our trust in the fullness of His glory (nature).

When Mary heard Elizabeth's words, she burst out in the song known to us as the *Magnificat*.[15] In this song we see Mary's deep faith in the very nature of God:

> My soul magnifies the Lord,
>> and my spirit rejoices in God my Savior!
>
> For He has looked with favor on the humble state of His
>> servant.
>> From now on all generations will call me blessed.
>
> For the Mighty One has done great things for me.
>> Holy is His name.
>
> His mercy extends to those who fear Him,
>> from generation to generation.
>
> He has performed mighty deeds with His arm;
>> He has scattered those who are proud
>> in the thoughts of their hearts.
>
> He has brought down rulers from their thrones,
>> but has exalted the humble.
>
> He has filled the hungry with good things,
>> but has sent the rich away empty.
>
> He has helped His servant Israel,
>> remembering to be merciful,
>
> as He promised to our fathers,
>> to Abraham and his descendants forever. (Luke 1:47-55)

Mary saw the living God as "the Mighty One." She knew He was *strong* enough to do what was best for her. And she knew He was *good* enough. He "filled the hungry with good things," and He remembered

---

[15] This name is based on the Latin word for "Magnify," which is the first word in the Latin version of the song.

to be "merciful, as He promised." Her faith pleased and honored God, and this is why God was pleased to honor her.

Joins Faith to the Words God Speaks

The great contrast between Mary and Zechariah is in how they responded to the word God spoke to them through the angel Gabriel. Mary joined faith to the message she heard from God, and but Zechariah did not.

We might ask how Zechariah could fail to have faith when the message was spoken so miraculously to him. Ultimately, only one thing mattered. Had he heard correctly from the Lord? If so, he had every reason to believe, and to live out his faith through our obedience, just as Mary did—and just as we all must do.

This points to the reason it is so important for us to understand how we can hear God's voice—and how we can know we have heard accurately. (This will be one of our highest priorities in Book Two: Growing in the Blessing.) If we can be sure we have heard accurately, this one thing remains: we must join our faith to God's word, as Mary did and as Zechariah did not.

Rejoices Even Before the Fulfillment Comes

Interestingly, Mary did not wait for the fulfillment of the promise to rejoice in God. Immediately, she went to the home of Elizabeth to share what God had spoken to her, and we simply can't miss the deep joy she expressed in her song of praise to God. This was long before Jesus' birth, which reveals another beautiful characteristic of the faith God blesses. If we know God has given us the promise, we don't have to wait for the promise to be fulfilled to rejoice. We can rejoice before the fulfillment, and our rejoicing is actually a demonstration of our faith.

Endures Until the Promise is Fulfilled

It's hard for us to imaging the unique challenges Mary faced as the mother of the Christ. To begin with, who would believe the story she told about her pregnancy? And we should not discount the difficulty of her journey to Bethlehem when Jesus' birth was so near. Most of all though, how difficult it was for her to witness the crucifixion of her own Son (John 19:25). How was she able to endure these things? Only because she believed the word God spoke to her, and she knew His promise would be fulfilled.

This is the faith we all must have if we are going to endure until God's promises are realized in our lives. We can be sure there will be challenges. When we obey, our circumstances may get worse before they get better (e.g. Ex. 5:22-23). How critical it is, then, to remember the promise God has given us.

Believes God will Bless—Even Me

Unfortunately, it's possible for us to believe God will bless in the general sense—without believing He will bless us. However, faith does not become dynamic and effective in our lives until we are able to say: "I believe God will bless *even me*." This is one of the characteristics we see in Mary. When she heard God's promise, she said, "…May it happen to me according to Your word (Luke 1:38)." Two of the most important words in her response are: "to me."

We see this same emphasis in the words Elizabeth spoke to her: "Blessed is she who has believed that the Lord's word to her will be fulfilled." Mary believed the words that were spoken "to her."

> *Mary did not have faith because she was Mary, she became Mary because she had faith.*

This is what made all the difference. Mary did not have faith because she was Mary, she became

Mary because she had faith. And you will become you when you have faith. Yes, you….

In the last chapter, we learned what it means to live in the fullness of God's blessing. To receive God's blessing is *good*, and to bless others is even *better*, and to bless God is the very *best*. As we think about each of these aspects of God's blessing, it's hard for us to imagine how anyone could have been more blessed than Mary.

To begin with, she was blessed by receiving the conception of the Son of God within her. Then, she became the instrument by which God's greatest blessing went out to the world. And because of the Son she bore, untold numbers have now bowed their knee to give thanks and praise to the God of heaven.

As we think about this, we must go back to the words Jesus spoke in Luke 11:28. When a woman in the crowd cried out, "Blessed is the womb that bore You, and blessed are the breasts that nursed You!"[16] Jesus replied by saying: "Blessed rather are those who hear the word of God and obey it."

The word "rather" in this verse is very important, not because it points away from Mary, but because it points to us. As blessed as Mary was, *anyone* who hears and obeys God's word can be blessed, just as she was. We, like her, can receive the Christ into our lives, and we can share Him with the world, with the result that others bow before the God of heaven and bring blessing to Him.

What then is necessary for this to happen? Just one thing. We, like Mary, must have the faith God blesses. Then, when we hear the word He speaks to us, we must say:

---

[16] Luke 1:27

May it happen to me according to Your word....

Summary

- God does not show favoritism, but He favors those who have faith.
- The faith God blesses:

    o   Trusts in His nature
    o   Joins faith to His word
    o   Rejoices when the promise is given
    o   Endures until the promise is fulfilled
    o   Believes God will bless—even me

- If only we can be sure we have heard God accurately, the one thing that remains for us is to obey and to trust in His blessing.
- Mary was greatly blessed, but this makes Jesus' words all the more impacting when He says, "Blessed rather [not just Mary] are those who hear and obey God's word (Luke 11:28)."

Discussion Questions
for Chapter 7

1. Are there ways God spoke to you through this chapter?

2. Based on the things we learned in this chapter about Mary, do you see her any differently now? If so, in what way?

3. What are some ways you are currently living by faith?

4. What characteristics of the faith God blesses do you need to grow in most?

5. Do you struggle to believe God can bless "even you"? If so, why do you think this is?

6. Are there some specific ways you believe God has spoken to you? Would you be willing to share these things with your group? Ask your group to pray that you will hear accurately and that you will have the faith to obey.

Assignment:

1. Memorize Mary's words in Luke 1:38. Let these words become the very attitude of your heart.

2. Position your heart to be ready to hear what God speaks to you. Carry this heart with you, and be ready to speak the words of Mary in Luke 1:38 when you recognize what God is speaking to you.

NOTES

NOTES

NOTES

NOTES

NOTES

NOTES

NOTES

NOTES

NOTES

NOTES

NOTES

NOTES